The

MAPLE LEAF ARMY

in Britain

PETER LONGSTAFF-TYRRELL

with

Patricia Berry

GOTE HOUSE PUBLISHING CO.

POLEGATE - EAST SUSSEX - UK

June 2003

The Maple Leaf Army in Britain.
Gote House Publishing Co. 2002.
PO Box 169, Polegate, East Sussex, UK.

ISBN 0-9521297-7-9

Cover: Deployment of Canadian forces, southern England and France 14 June 1940.

British Library Cataloguing in Publication Data.
A catalogue record for this book is available from the British Library.

www.gotemilitaria.co.uk

Typeset in 11 on 13pt Garamond ITC.
Origination by Gote House, BN26 6BS.

Research by Peter Longstaff-Tyrrell

That Peace in Our Time
The artefacts of WWII in Sussex
ISBN 0-952197-0-1 (1993)

Operation Cuckmere Haven
Military aspects of the Cuckmere Valley
ISBN 0-9521297-1-X (1997)

A Sussex Sunset
RAF Pevensey & RAF Wartling Radar, 1938-1964
ISBN 0-9521297-2-8 (1998)

Tyrrell's List
The artefacts of Two Great Wars in Sussex
ISBN 0-9521297-3-6 (1999)

Destination Fowington
East Sussex military airfields & Allied aircraft incidents
ISBN 0-9521297-4-4 (1999)

Front-Line Sussex
Napoleon Bonaparte to the Cold War
ISBN 0-7509-2592-2 (2000)

The Seaford Mutiny of 1795
The Royal Oxfordshire Militia rebellion
ISBN 0-9521297-6-0 (2000)

Barracks to Bunkers
250 years of military activity in Sussex
ISBN 0-7509-2908-1 (2002)

The Maple Leaf Army in Britain
ISBN 0-9521297-7-9 (2002)

Reflections from the Cuckmere Valley
ISBN 0-9521297-8-7. January 2003.

Author's introduction

Traditional family and military ties between Canada and the British Isles are deep-rooted, beyond the emigration programmes of the nineteenth century. At first Canada was mainly largely settled by the French and was ceded to Great Britain in 1763. During that period the only permanent settlements flourished in the eastern territories. In 1875 the entire population, excluding Indians, amounted to about four million people. Settlers traded mainly in forestry, seal-oil and furs. Lower Canada was primarily French and Upper Canada predominantly British.

The 1867 British North America Act united both territories into a single legislative confederation that became the Dominion of Canada. This hereditary theme is reflected in the titles of the Non-Permanent Active Militia Regiments listed herein. With the outbreak of the First World War Canadian Army divisions were mobilised from former servicemen and militia units to serve alongside Britain. Four Canadian divisions served with distinction between 1914-1919 - as the country emerged as a nation in their own recognition.

With the dawning of the Second World War dominion troops again fully supported the motherland. The first convoy of Canadian troops docked in Liverpool on 19 December 1939 and they were followed by the initial squadron of the Royal Canadian Air Force on 25 February 1940. Records relate that 500,000 Canadian armed services people served part of their Second World War years in Britain. Also some 40,000 British/Canadian marriages resulted and it has been reckoned that between 7,000 and 8,000 former Canadian armed services personnel settled in Sussex after the Second World War. One comment was if the need ever arose again there was no need to send men, just send over the uniforms.

Briefly in mid-1941 the 2nd Canadian Division exchanged roles with a British division protecting part of the Sussex coast. That autumn Canadian Corps wholly relinquished their role as GHQ Reserve and moved into Sussex. Soon after the Corps was taken over by Major-General H.D.G. Crerar, the dynamic Anglo-Irishman, with Lt-General Bernard Montgomery in charge of the command.

The following years became a period of endeavour and toil, of arduous training and exercises, of frustrations and inactivity, then experiencing great tragedy. A time of close liaison with the English communities and the countryside, leading to postwar friendships and numerous war bride situations. Tales from this period have become legend . . .

For this study the coastal communities between Brighton and Hastings, inland at the Ashdown Forest, westerly around Horsham, plus Operation *Spartan* towards Oxford, are particularly focused for attention as Canadian troops largely occupied Sussex during the Second World War.

This previously untold Commemoration of the life and varied times of civilians and Canadian armed service personnel during two world wars is archived often in their own verbatim. Official and civilian accounts, correspondence, photographs and memorabilia, collated with period news reports and regimental extracts, complete this exclusive and timely account as *The Maple Leaf Army in Britain*.

Peter Longstaff-Tyrrell, Polegate, East Sussex. July 2002.

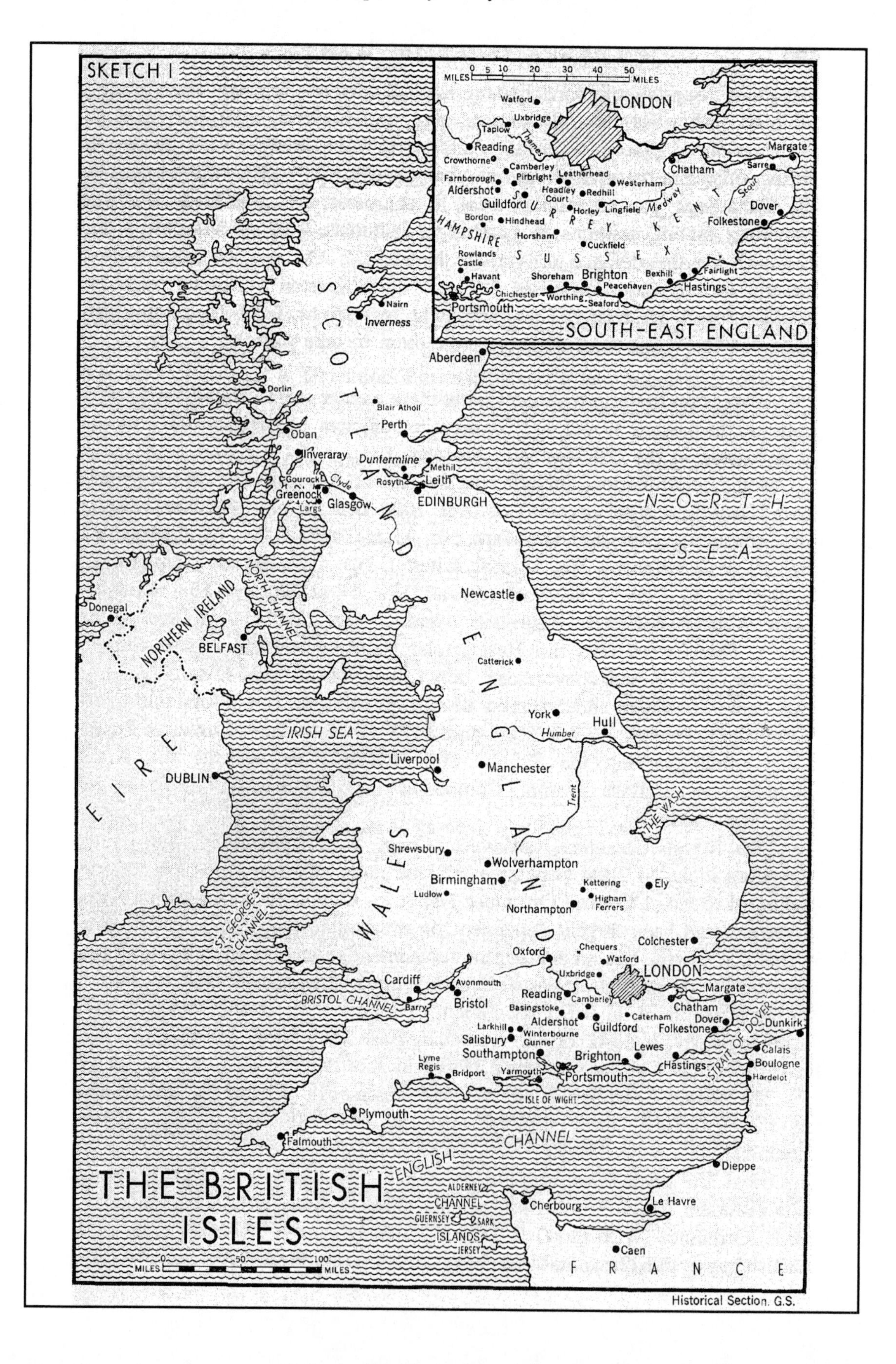
SKETCH 1
THE BRITISH ISLES
SOUTH-EAST ENGLAND
LONDON
SCOTLAND
ENGLAND
WALES
NORTHERN IRELAND
EIRE
NORTH SEA
IRISH SEA
NORTH CHANNEL
ST. GEORGE'S CHANNEL
BRISTOL CHANNEL
ENGLISH CHANNEL
STRAIT OF DOVER
CHANNEL ISLANDS
FRANCE
Historical Section. G.S.

Contents

With our best wishes for
Christmas 1939
May God bless you & protect you.
Elizabeth R George R.I.

The Maple Leaf Forever

In the days of yore, from Britain's shore,
Wolfe, the dauntless here came,
And planted firm Britannia's flag
On Canada's fair domain'
He may it wave, our boast, our pride,
And joined in love together,
The Thistle, Shamrock, Rose entwine,
The Maple Leaf forever.

Chorus
The Maple Leaf, our emblem dear,
The Maple Leaf forever,
God save our King, and Heaven bless
The Maple Leaf forever.

O Canada

O Canada! our home and native land!
True patriot - love in all thy sons command.
With glowing hearts we see thee rise,
The True North, strong and free,
And stand on guard, O Canada,
We stand on guard for thee.
O Canada, glorious and free!
We stand on guard, we stand on guard for thee,
O Canada, we stand on guard for thee!

O Canada! Where pines and maples grow,
Great prairies spread and lordly rivers flow,
How dear to us thy broad domain,
From East to Western Sea.
Thou land of hope for all who toil!
Thou True North, strong and free!

O Canada! Beneath thy shining skies,
May stalwart sons and gentle maidens rise,
To keep thee steadfast through the years,
From East to Western Sea,
Our beloved native land!
Our True North, strong and free.

THE FIRST WORLD WAR

Britain's nineteenth century emigration links with the New World fluctuated with the domestic economy in the motherland. Changes in farming methods, machinery and merchandising, led to a surplus of discontented labour. A flow of manpower to industrial areas followed, along with families that sought fresh opportunities overseas. Australia and New Zealand were particularly popular and then in the decade prior to 1914 emigration to Canadian territories became an attractive proposition for hundreds of families, despite harrowing conditions travelling and settling in undeveloped towns and countryside.

A census of 1890 indicates that there were more than 90,000 British-born farmers in the USA and in excess of 100,000 British-born farm labourers. Many of this migrant community had first arrived in Canada and then branched out to seek pastures new, in agriculture and industry. Most mid nineteenth-century Highland emigrants went to Upper Canada (Ontario) initially. The district by 1850 was erratically populated with Scotch-Canadian settlements that perpetuated British traditions.

With the British government declaring war with Germany in August 1914 Canada was realistically at war with the Hun also. Canadian constitutional ties with Britain rendered the Dominion with no option whether to fight alongside the motherland and there was never any doubt that Canada would serve fully-committed with Britain. Prime Minister Robert Borden conveyed their devotion to the nation in a special war session on 18 August 1914. He announced . . . As to our duty we are all agreed we stand shoulder to shoulder with Britain and the other Dominions in this quarrel. And that our duty we shall not fail to fulfil as the honour of Canada demands.

At that time however the regular army in Canada comprised of just 3,000 men, serving in two cavalry regiments as the Permanent Active Militia. These troops served as The Royal Canadian Dragoons and Lord Strathcona's Horse, together with an infantry battalion of the Royal Canadian Regiment (RCR) plus some artillery, engineers and service supporting units. However within a few days of the declaration of war this nominal force was bolstered by a new infantry regiment known as The Princess Patricia's Canadian Light Infantry (PPCLI). They took their name from the daughter of the Governor-General of Canada, HRH Prince Arthur The Duke of Connaught.

The regiment was raised by Captain Hamilton Gault who personally provided 100,000 dollars to fund the regiment. His plan was to utilise former servicemen and this policy swiftly enrolled veterans from across the nation. In under three weeks the regiment was at full strength, with almost all of the troops having served beforehand and some 90% of them being born in the UK. In all 1,098 men were selected from some 3,000 applying for military service. Interestingly regimental records show that every regiment of the regular British Army was represented on battalion parade, with just one British regiment being the exception amongst this new force.

As part of 80th Brigade, of the newly-created 27th Division, the PPCLI became the first Canadian battalion crossing to France and serving in the front-line. These men of the PPCLI were in good company as most of the 27th were seasoned regulars returning from overseas duty in Hong Kong, Tientsin and India.

Prewar Canadian plans to utilise reservists from the 60,000 strong Non-Permanent Active Militia (NPAM) represented the nation from a wealth of cities and towns named for posterity. Amongst three Military Districts with six Divisional Areas the NPAM consisted of 36 cavalry regiments and 106 infantry regiments.

Volunteers with previous military training and service records from regional militia forces formed a body that was promptly welcomed by the British authorities. An infantry division of 25,000 men, formed on British lines, would provide ample reserve units. Alas this prewar plan did not take its course and an almost chaotic assembly, led by Colonel Sam Hughes, the volatile Minister of Militia, dictated a complex and cumbersome formation of divisions that began to assemble for embarkation from Quebec on 25 September 1914.

Finally, amid the disarray of troop movements, mid-afternoon on 3 October 1914 the main force of 30 vessels set sail ferrying 30,605 officers and men, with 6,816 horses, 127 guns, 595 motor and horse-drawn vehicles and all of 82 bicycles listed.

Of the first contingent to go overseas from Canada it was later determined that 18,495 troops had been born in the British Isles and just 9,159 were born in Canada. The convoy was joined at the entrance to the St Lawrence by the SS *Canada* with the 2nd Lincolns on board, after serving in Bermuda, and a couple of days later by the SS *Florizel* off Cape Race with 539 officers and men from Newfoundland. The SS *Manhattan* had sailed off alone two days after the main force with 863 horses, 90 motors and 130 horse-drawn carts and reserves of stores that had been left over from the initial departures.

Major Fell and Lt John Cosgrove of the 6th Field Company were amongst those volunteers had gone to Valcartier Camp, Quebec. Fell commanded and both were included in the 1st Field Company which sailed. Travers Cosgrove recalls . . . Great cheers rang out across the ocean when the New Foundland contingent came out to join the convoy. The constancy of the British battleship and smaller vessels, which guarded the convoy, remained imbedded in my father's mind throughout his life. Always on station! He would call a trusted friend *The British Battleship.* The gallant Major Fell is remembered in Vancouver by Fell Road.

The Canadian troops were meant to land at Southampton, but the sea journey was curtailed at Plymouth on account of U-boat threats in the English Channel. After the near shambles boarding the troops in Quebec it took nine days to disembark the men, equipment and their supplies before the divisions were transferred to the dubious winter delights of Salisbury Plain in southern England.

By August 1916 four Canadian divisions were serving with distinction in France. The landmark battle at Vimy Ridge in April 1917, where all four Canadian divisions fought alongside, was the pinnacle of the Dominion's fighting achievements. At the signing of the Peace Treaties the nation emerged into recognition with an individual signature on the agreements and a separate seat at The League of Nations.

The official records of the Canadian Corps reveal that of 619,636 men and women who served 51,748 were killed in action or perished of their wounds. Some 7,796 died from disease, injury or illness, totalling at 59,544 fatalities. The overall figure of First World War Canadian Army casualties, of all kinds, amassed at 232,494. Victoria Cross awards went to 64 Canadians, including six to men of the Canadian Cavalry Brigade and men serving with the RFC or RAF. A total of 13,190 Military Medals were awarded amongst 21,763 other British honours and decorations to Canadians.

PLT.

INTERNATIONAL ASSOCIATIONS

In about 1910 my grandfather's brothers Walter and Ernest Washford, in their early twenties, went to seek their fortune in Canada. Ernest returned to England, but Walter remained and joined the Canadian Army after the outbreak of war. He saw action on the Western Front, was wounded, and ended up at one of the Epsom camps. This was about three miles across the Downs from the Belmont home of my grandfather and his family.

At Epsom Walter and a fellow Canuck named James Y. Waldrum became pals and they regularly walked to Belmont. They were repatriated, but, Jimmy (from Hope Street, Toronto) returned in July 1936. I think he was a veteran of the Vimy Ridge action when four divisions of the Canadian Corps, on 9th-10th April 1917, took the 61-metre high ridge held by the enemy since October 1914.

Jimmy was en route to France for the dedication of the Vimy Ridge memorial, commemorating the 66,000 Canadians killed or missing in the war. He sent my grandparents this photograph of the occasion. He enclosed a one dollar bill for me (then aged seven). I got five shillings for it at the bank and bought my first fountain pen.

Pat Hennessy, Epsom, Surrey. July 2002.

Dedication of the Vimy Ridge memorial in 1936. (Pat Hennessy)

HOME THOUGHTS FROM ABROAD

You asked me if the people dress odd. In answer, why they dressed in costumes as in Canada and you would never know the difference, only this is a larger city than they have in Canada. The country over here is very hilly and is splendid land for farming. The fields instead of having fences are bound in by small green hedges, present a picturesque sight, with oxen etc farming to a large extent here in place of horses.

I am sending you my picture, I did not take very good, owing to the negative being too dark and besides I was very tired from traversing London. As news is scarce I will close with loads of love to you, Chubb and the kiddies. I am your loving brother.

Private E.A. Henry, No 1093373, 254th Battalion Draft D Company Platoon. Seaford Camp, Sussex.

BRITISH SUMMER TIME

It is just seven-thirty our time and it would be about two o'clock in Hillier now, but the time is one hour later than it really should be on account of the light-saving system in England.

The clocks have been moved on one hour so people can go to bed one hour earlier. By the system of lighting it is not dark until 10.15, so we generally go to bed before it gets dark. One disadvantage here is roll call at 9.30, so one cannot get to bed until after that time, no matter how much sleep he wished. Reveille is generally at 5.30am, so you will see this makes quite a long day. *Corporal Simmon, Seaford Camp. 10 August 1917.*

SEAFORD CEMETERY COMMEMORATION

High on a Sussex hill, with glimpses of the grey English Channel through the trees to the south, a group of people stood in the winter sunshine to pay tribute to 191 Canadian soldiers who died three-quarters of a century ago. It was Miss Mary Ellis, a life-long resident of Seaford who alerted the Canadian Veterans Association to the fact that these men, who died from wounds and illness suffered in the First World War had lain ever since far home in the Alfriston Road cemetery at Seaford.

Initiated by Bob Baxter, then Canadian Veterans Association UK President and a Sussex resident, with Seaford British Legion and background provided by Seaford Museum, the inaugural Service of Commemoration began beside the cemetery's military memorial. In the presence of local dignitaries, standards from branches of CVAUK and the Royal British Legion paraded, billowing in the sea breeze, as bugler Sid Turner sounded the Last Post. Silence was observed, Reveille sounded and poppy wreaths laid after which the party had time to walk past the immaculate Commonwealth War Graves Commission plots.

En route to St Leonards parish church the group went past rising ground where the wooden huts of North Camp once stood. At the church they inspected a pair of brass dedication plates at the two front pews, presented in 1919 by Canadian servicemen who worshiped there. The church memorials are shaped like maple leafs and bear the inscriptions . . . This bench and frontal were presented to the church in grateful memory of its services by Canadian troops encamped here during the last two years of the Great War.

Some of the casualties died from wounds, but many succumbed to the terrible influenza epidemic which swept the world after the guns were silenced. They should have gone home, but were delayed in Seaford into 1919 due to the shortage of shipping.

Patricia Berry reviewed the inaugural Canadian Veterans Pilgrimage, Seaford. November 1994.

FOR WHOM THE BELL TOLLS

During repairs to the belfry at Litlington church, near Seaford, it was noted that some of the redundant wooden mechanism bore signatures with dates. These rewarded a closer examination with a hand-lamp and magnifying glass. Some of the names may have been Sussex craftsmen who worked on the belfry long ago. However, perhaps most intriguing are the signatures of Canadians and other soldiers who were in Litlington in the First World War. Eric Jones No 107343 and P. Haponder 10745? signed 30 June 1917. Only Eric Jones gave his address as Victoria, British Columbia. Both men were of the 2nd Battalion, The Canadian Regiment.

We also noted M.E. Kerr and H.A. Clarke who both seem to have been with the 8th Battalion, Clarke dated his inscription 2 May 1919. We also found a B. Horton and ? Russell, no dates, but they wrote "Canadian Army". A few other names are members of British regiments. A. Moore, A. Hayes, R. Fosket and S. Ford, left no record of their origins but their marks on the woodwork makes one suspect they too may have been Canadians from the 8th Battalion. There is also a May Jones - apparently out with the soldiers exploring the countryside. They may have been stationed at the very large camp at Seaford in the area which is now Upper Belgrave Road - hence the name North Camp Road that joins it.

A later signatory on 17 October 1935 is C.W.A. Tigenvast who prophetically inscribed alongside the Canadians, "Will there be another war?" Well there was another war and Canadians dutifully returned to our county in volume. Notably though, if any troops found their way through the very low door up the dark stone staircase to Litlington bell chamber, they left no record of their visit.

Sir Alan Leslie, Alfriston, East Sussex. July 2002.

From his report in Cuckmere News, November 1993.

The sombre scene at Seaford Cemetery where 191 young Canadians and 19 West Indian soldiers are commemorated many having died from influenza whilst waiting shipment back home. (Gote House)

AN INTERNATIONAL TRAGEDY

Spanish Flu was the name given to mysterious and disastrous epidemic that killed more people throughout the world than the Great War itself. The sceptic influenza suddenly began its ravages in early in 1918, further upsurges arose in the winter of 1918-1919.

In a single year 20 million people perished from the disease, some 16 million of them in India. In Europe 166,000 deaths happened in France. In Germany 225,000 people were struck down and in Britain 229,000 people were claimed. This compares with 1,500 civilian and 750,000 war dead in the previous four years.

Most of its victims were young men; cemeteries on Salisbury Plain are the last resting place of scores of young Australian and New Zealand soldiers, too late for the Western Front. Three quarters of our population were struck down and public meeting places like cafes and cinemas were closed.

The effects for many were far more devastating than four years of global warfare. Then the epidemic disappeared just as dramatically as it developed.

From Blighty Brighton, *QueenSpark Books, 1991.*

UNCLE TOM SOLDIERING ON . . .

Papers inherited concerning my late 'uncle' Tom Simmons (grandmother's lover!) reveal just part of his colourful military life-style.

Thomas Alfred Simmons was born 26 June 1897 in Lewes, although he spent his early years in Canada. He had the distinction of serving in both World Wars. He enrolled as Private 100181 with the 66th Battalion Canadian Expeditionary Force, and served up to 29 March 1919. Period photographs and documents from his tour of duty show him on 15

November 1915 at Edburton with No 3 Company 66th O Battalion, plus later his discharge papers.

During World War Two 'uncle Tom' served as Sapper L-12181, Royal Canadian Engineers, South Saskatchewan Regiment, from 27 September 1939 to 15 September 1945. Again a variety of personal effects have been passed through our family.

Apparently Tom Simmons had been married in Canada, but returned to Lewes soon after his discharge in 1945. He finally got divorced from his Canadian wife in 1972. His medals have long since disappeared, but there is reference to the Canadian Volunteer Service Medal and Clasp in our family.

Steve Steggall, Lewes. April 2002.

Thomas Alfred Simmons, seen opposite, served with the South Saskatchewan Regiment to March 1919 and then from September 1939 until September 1945 when he was 47-years old and settled back in Lewes.

(Steve Steggall)

CANADIAN EXPEDITIONARY FORCE

Discharge Certificate

This is to Certify that No. 10018[illegible] (Rank) Private

Name (in full) Thomas Alfred SIMMONS enlisted in

WAR DIARY
or
~~INTELLIGENCE SUMMARY.~~
(*Erase heading not required.*)

Army Form C. 2118.

Instructions regarding War Diaries and Intelligence Summaries are contained in F. S. Regs., Part II. and the Staff Manual respectively. Title pages will be prepared in manuscript.

Place	Date	Hour	Summary of Events and Information	Remarks and references to Appendices
LONDON, ONTARIO.	16/8/16		Inspection of Unit by G.O.C., No.1 Military District and A.D.M.S., No.1 Military District.	E.S.
"	16/8/16		Inspection of Orderly Room Records by Officers of Headquarters Staff, No.1 Mil.District.	
"	16/8/16		1500 Cases of Ordnance and Red Cross Supplies forwarded to Montreal for shipment to England.	E.S.
"	16/8/16		1 Recruit taken on the Strength, bringing Unit to exact strength of Establishment, viz.,- OFFICERS - 14, OTHER RANKS - 118.	
"	18/6/16	12.20 P.M.	Complete Unit comprising Lt.Col.E.SEABORN, Major C.E.BROWN, Major J.C.WILSON, Captains J.S.HUDSON, A.TURNER, E.H.YOUNG, J.MORIARTY, E.BICE, A.E.FRALEIGH, R.H.HENDERSON, C.L.DOUGLAS, C.P.JENTO, G.M.BROCK, and Lieut.J.A.DICKIE, and 118 OTHER RANKS entrained at Grand Trunk Railway Station.	E.S.
HALIFAX, N.S.	21/8/16.	9 AM.	Unit arrived at HALIFAX, N.S.	E.S.
"	21/8/16.	11 AM.	Unit embarked on H.M.T.2810 (Olympic)	E.S.
"	21/8/16		Lt.Colonel E.SEABORN appointed Principal Medical Officer of the ship.	
"	21/8/16		Troop Hospital on board taken over by Unit, commenced treatment of all cases of sickness which developed and continued same throughout voyage.	E.S.
"	24/8/16		1 Other Rank of Unit transferred to Shore Hospital, HALIFAX, seriously ill.	E.S.
"	24/8/16		Inspection of Troops and Ship by H.R.H. the Duke of Connaught.	
"	24/8/16.	12.30 P.M.	Ship proceeded from Halifax.	E.S.
LIVERPOOL	30/8/16.	10.00 A.M.	Unit disembarked at LIVERPOOL.	E.S.
"	30/8/16.	10.30 A.M.	Unit entrained for SHORNCLIFFE.	
SHORNCLIFFE.	30/8/16.	9 P.M.	Unit arrived at SHORNCLIFFE Station, and proceeded to camp.	E.S.
"	30/8/16	10 P.M.	Unit arrived at Canvas Camp, St Martin's Plain, SHORNCLIFFE, KENT.	E.S.
"	31/8/16.		Unit attached to No.8 Canadian Stationary Hospital, St Martin's Plain, for Quarters and Rations.	E.S.
"	31/8/16		One Casualty having occurred En Route, Strength at this date was - OFFICERS - 14. OTHER RANKS - 117.	E.S.

Edwin Seaborn Lt.Colonel,
Cmdg. No 10 Canadian Stationary Hospital.

A6943 Wt. W11422/M1160 350,000 12/16 D. D. & L. Forms/C. 2118/14.

War Diary extracts relating to Seaford and Shorncliffe Barracks hospital activity. (Patricia Berry)

(8)

WAR DIARY
or
~~INTELLIGENCE SUMMARY.~~
(*Erase heading not required.*)

Army Form C. 211

Instructions regarding War Diaries and Intelligence Summaries are contained in F. S. Regs., Part II. and the Staff Manual respectively. Title pages will be prepared in manuscript.

Place	Date	Hour	Summary of Events and Information	Remarks and references to Appendices
SHORNCLIFFE KENT.	1/11/16.	2PM.	Letter received from A.D.M.S., Canadian Training Division, SHORNCLIFFE, directing that Lt.Colonel E.SEABORN, two Medical Officers, Quartermaster and 35 Other Ranks report to D.A.D.M.S., Canadians, SEAFORD, for the purpose of taking over Raven's Croft Military Hospital.	ADMS.CT T-V-6.0 d/1/11/
"	2/11/16.		Lt.Colonel E.SEABORN, Major J.C.WILSON, Capt. A.E.FRALEIGH and 20 Other Ranks recalled from Command.	E.S.
"	2/11/16.	9AM.	Lt.Colonel E.SEABORN, Major J.C.WILSON, Captains A.E.FRALEIGH and G.M.BROCK, Lieut.J.A. DICKIE and 33 Other Ranks proceeded by rail to SEAFORD, SUSSEX.	E.S.
SEAFORD, SUSSEX.	2/11/16.	6PM.	Details as above arrived at SEAFORD Station and marched to CHYNGTON CAMP (1 Mile East)	E.S.
	2/11/16		Unit attached to 103rd Battalion, C.E.F., for Quarters and Rations.	E.S.
"	3/11/16		1 Other Rank recalled from Command.	
"	5/11/16		Raven's Croft Military Hospital taken over through Board of Survey from Imperial authorities and established as Headquarters of Unit. Bed capacity approximately 100. About 75 Imperial patients in Hospital at time of taking over were treated until their recovery or transfer to Imperial Hospitals. Chyngton Camp in its earliest stages as a Canadian Camp at this date, about three Battalions being quartered there in hutments. Raven's Croft Hospital a School building but occupied by the R.A.M.C., as a Military Hospital since 1914.	E.S.
"	8/11/16		1 Other Rank recalled from Command.	E.S.
"	11/11/16.		2 Other Ranks recalled from Command.	
"	13/11/16		Captain C.P.JENTO and 1 Other Rank recalled from Command.	E.S.
"	25/11/16		Nursing Sisters A.HICKS, J.MACALLUM and A.E.WHITELY taken on the Strength on transfer from Duchess of Connaught's Canadian Red Cross Hospital, TAPLOW.	E.S.
"	25/11/16		Nursing Sister E.ORME taken on the Strength on transfer from Moore Barracks Canadian Hospital, SHORNCLIFFE.	E.S.
"	25/11/16		Nursing Sisters S.B.POPHAM and B.M.WILSON taken on the strength on transfer from Canadian Red Cross Special Hospital, BUXTON.	E.S.
"	28/11/16.		1 Other Rank struck off Strength on transfer to Moore Barracks Canadian Hospital, SHORNCLIFFE.	E.S.
"	30/11/16		1 Other Rank taken on Strength on transfer from C.A.M.C.Training School, SHORNCLIFFE.	E.S.
"	30/11/16		Many new Battalions arrived in camp direct from Canada during the month. A high rate of sickness developed amongst these new arrivals, due largely to the unaccustomed dampness of the English climate.	E.S.

A6943 Wt. W11422/M1160 350,000 12/16 D. D. & L. Forms/C. 2118/14.

PIONEERING LINKS OVERSEAS

My late father, Major John Robert Cosgrove DSO, MC, Member of the Engineering Institute of Canada, was with 6th Field Company RCE prior to 1914 and arrived with the Canadian Expeditionary Force at Plymouth at the end of October 1914. They caught their breath on Salisbury Plain, before being ferried to St Nazaire in February 1915.

The Canadian Engineers occupied part of the Royal Engineers training camp at Shorncliffe near Folkestone, preparing for the real thing - much as I did 25 years on. From early 1916 JRC seems to have done a spell at Shorncliffe, putting into practical training what he had experienced at Flanders as Lt J.R. Cosgrove and where won his Military Cross. He has carefully titled many of his collection of over 175 photographs from that time.

In the winter of 1916-1917, while the British and Canadian Army was bogged down and could not get ammunition forward, Sappers endeavoured to repair the road system that was falling apart. They thought of light railways, but how could they get men to operate them? The Canadians responded that half their men, already in Europe, were volunteers from their railroad network. The Canadian railway troops were promptly formed from men and the British followed suit. My father had some experience from railway work with Robert McAlpine & Sons before he left Scotland in 1910 and he was appointed to command the 7th Battalion. He was later awarded the DSO for their remarkable speed in advancing under orders. He returned to Canada late in 1919.

My mother had reached Canada about the same time as father, but only got to Vancouver in early 1914. She returned on an American vessel and they were married in May 1915 on his first leave at Plymouth. She was soon appointed matron of a military hospital in Sussex and, alas, had to give up when the building was mistakenly bombed by the Germans and she was injured. I was born in Vancouver in October 1920 and served with the British Royal Engineers.

Travers Cosgrove, Huntly, Aberdeenshire. June 2002.

Opposite: Officers clear a make-shift footbridge on the Royal Military Canal at Hythe, May 1916. (Travers Cosgrove)

Lower: Major Cosgrove finds time to relax in a gun emplacement trench near Ploegsteert in Belgium. (Travers Cosgrove)

BASE BALL

A Professional ..

Base Ball Match

Between the

165th v. 167th

CANADIAN SIEGE BATTERIES

Will be played on the

FOOTBALL GROUND

Brighton Road, Horsham, on

Saturday Next, July 15, 1916

At 2.30 p.m. sharp.

Admission - 3d.

Proceeds for Patriotic Purposes.

Corpl. ORANGE, G.V. Manager

PRINTED BY THE HORSHAM PRESS, PARK STREET.

Canadians soon introduced their life-style to English civilians. Indeed many soldiers became reunited with family members from descendants who had emigrated years previously. This mid-1916 base ball contest at Horsham typifies the blending. *(Horsham Museum)*

The 1st Canadian Machine Gun Corps on parade at Seaford in March 1919. The location is thought to be Chyngton Road bordering the golf-course. (Patricia Berry)

Lower: Canadian Army Service Corps and Engineers camps at Seaford 1918. Decorative insignia added distinctive pride to their units. (Patricia Berry)

The cinema at the Epsom Canadian Convalescent Camp helped renew some qualities of life for inmates. (Patricia Berry)

Middle: The sombre setting at Pond Farm, Woodcote Road, Epsom. (Patricia Berry)

Lower: The recreation hall and hutting at the former Woodcote Park Convalescent Camp in Epsom. (Patricia Berry)

NON-PERMANENT ACTIVE MILITIA REGIMENTS - AUGUST 1914

CAVALRY.

The Governor General's Body Guard.

1st	Hussars
2nd	Dragoons
3rd	The Prince of Wales's Canadian Dragoons
4th	Hussars.
5th	Princess Louise Dragoon Guards.
6th	Duke of Connaught's Royal Canadian Hussars.
7th	Hussars.
8th	Princess Louise's New Brunswick Hussars.
9th	Mississauga Horse.
10th	No regiment with this number.
11th	Hussars.
12th	Manitoba Dragoons.
13th	Scottish Light Dragoons.
14th	King's Canadian Hussars.
15th	Light Horse.
16th	Light Horse.
17th	Duke of York's Royal Canadian Hussars.
18th	Mounted Rifles.
19th	Alberta Dragoons.
20th	Border Horse.
21st	Alberta Horse.
22nd	Saskatchewan Light Horse.
23rd	Alberta Rangers.
24th	Grey's Horse.
25th	Brant Dragoons.
26th	Stanstead Dragoons.
27th	Light Horse.
28th	New Brunswick Dragoons.
29th	Light Horse.
30th	British Columbia Horse.
31st	British Columbia Horse.
32nd	Manitoba Horse.
33rd	Vaudreuil and Soulanges Hussars. - Disbanded 1 October 1914.
34th	Fort Garry Horse.
35th	Central Alberta Horse.
36th	Prince Edward Island Light Horse.

INFANTRY

The Governor General's Body Guard.

1st	Canadian Grenadier Guards.
2nd	Queen's Own Rifles of Canada.
3rd	Victoria Rifles of Canada.
4th	Chasseurs Canadiens.
5th	Royal Highlanders of Canada.
6th	Duke of Connaught's Own Rifles.
7th	Fusiliers.
8th	Royal Rifles.
9th	Voltigeurs de Quebec.
10th	Royal Grenadiers.
11th	Irish Fusiliers of Canada.
12th	York Rangers.
13th	Royal Regiment.
14th	Princess of Wales's Own Rifles.
15th	Argyll Light Infantry.
16th	Prince Edward.
17th	Regiment of Infantry.
18th	Francs-Tireurs de Saguenay.
19th	Lincoln.
20th	Halton Rifles.
21st	Essex Fusiliers.
22nd	Oxford Rifles.
23rd	Northern Pioneers.
24th	Kent.
25th	Regiment.
26th	Middlesex Light Infantry.
27th	Lambton (St Clair Borderers).
28th	Perth.
29th	Waterloo. Redesignated Highland Light Infantry of Canada 15 April 1915.
30th	Wellington Rifles.
31st	Grey.
32nd	Bruce.
33rd	Huron.
34th	Ontario.
35th	Simcoe Foresters.
36th	Peel.
37th	Haldimand Rifles.
38th	Dufferin Rifles of Canada.
39th	Norfolk Rifles.
40th	Northumberland.

41st Brockville Rifles.
42nd Lanark and Renfrew.
43rd Duke of Cornwall's Own Rifles.
44th Lincoln and Welland.
45th Victoria and Haliburton.
46th Durham.
47th Frontenac.
48th Highlanders.
49th Hastings Rifles.
50th Victoria.
51st Soo Rifles.
52nd Prince Albert Volunteers.
53rd Sherbrooke.
54th Carabineers de Sherbrooke.
55th Megantic Light Infantry disbanded 3 Sept 1912, re-formed as 55th Infantry 29 Aug 1914.
56th Grenville.
57th Peterborough Rangers.
58th 58th Westmount Rifles formed 2 Nov 1914. Previously 58th Compton Regiment, converted to cavalry as 7th Hussars 1 May 1903.
59th Stormont and Glengarry.
60th 60th Rifles of Canada.
61st Montmagny and L'Islet.
62nd Saint John Fusiliers.
63rd Halifax Rifles.
64th Chateauguay and Beauharnois.
65th Carabiniers Mont Royal.
66th Princess Louise Fusiliers.
67th Carleton Light Infantry.
68th Early Grey's Own Rifles.
69th Annapolis.
70th 70th Colchester & Hants renumbered 76th 2 May 1910, 70th Regiment formed 7 Aug 1914.
71st York.
72nd Seaforth Higlanders of Canada.
73rd Northumberland.
74th New Brunswick Rangers.
75th Lunenburg.
76th Colchester and Hants Rifles.
77th Wentworth.
78th Pictou (Highlanders)
79th Cameron Highlanders of Canada.
80th Nicolet.
81st Hants.
82nd Abgeweit Light Infantry.
83rd Joliet.
84th St Hyacinthe.
85th Regiment.
86th Three Rivers Regiment disbanded 1 April 1914, re-formed 1 Oct 1915.
87th Quebec.
88th Victoria Fusiliers.
89th Temiscouata and Rimouski.
90th Winnipeg Rifles.
91st Canadian Highlanders.
92nd Dorchester.
93rd Cumberland.
94th Victoria (Argyll Higlanders)
95th Saskatchewan Rifles.
96th Lake Superior.
97th Algonquin Rifles.
98th Infantry.
99th Manitoba Rangers.
100th Winnipeg Grenadiers.
101st Edmonton Fusiliers.
102nd Rocky Mountain Rangers.
103rd Calgary Rifles.
104th Westminster Fusiliers of Canada.
105th Sasatoon Fusiliers.
106th Winnipeg.
107th East Kootenay.

The Canadian Air Force Takes Off

Associations with Shoreham aerodrome encompass both World Wars. Early records show the victim of a fatal accident on 4 February 1915, during training, was Canadian Lt William Sharpe. His Maurice Farman aircraft side-slipped, diving into a field between the *Sussex Pad* Hotel and Lancing College. This incident led to the Headmaster at Lancing College banning pupils from flying activities, although no doubt youthful impressions of aircraft close-by has influenced generations of pupils at the Gothic college.

The training of new pilots increased rapidly as the demand grew. Two new training schools were established in Britain, together with the formation of Reserve squadrons in Canada. Pilots were accepted at the rate of 1,300 per month, although a flying course consisted of just 18 hours including two night landings and a 60-mile cross-country flight.

In late April 1919 No 1 Wing Canadian Air Force transited from Upper Heyford in Oxfordshire to Shoreham. Led by the famous former RNAS pilot Lt-Colonel R. Leckie, the Wing comprised of No 1 Squadron with venerable SE5a bi-planes and No 2 Squadron with de Havilland 9a bombers. No 1 Squadron had been created as a training unit at Gosport in 1917 and in late November 1918 it became Canadian Air Force fighter No 1 Squadron.

On 22 May 1919 Major Carter DSO, MC, the No 2 Squadron CO, was involved in a fatal crash flying a re-built Fokker D.VII. The top wing of the fighter folded and the aircraft plummeted into a field near the college. Sadly Major Carter joined other airmen in Shoreham Old Cemetery who had perished after taking-off from the aerodrome.

Resources from the Canadian authorities dwindled to such an extent that the Wing resident at Shoreham was wound down during 1919. No 1 Squadron had been supplied with Sopwith Dolphins, but they were disbanded on 28 January 1920. Then during February that year the Wing HQ and No 2 Squadron followed suit. This left the Packing Section to close-up activities after official CAF operations ceased. Included in the functions was the matter of 65 captured German aircraft. These aircraft had been collated at Shoreham after the war and had subsequently been donated to the CAF by the British Government. However the Canadian authorities abandoned their plans for a postwar air force. Finally in December 1921 the CAF Packaging Section at Shoreham completed their dutiful task and left for Christmas back home.

Shoreham's grass airfield then in use lay dormant, variously it was offered for sale until it went back to cattle grazing. Flying returned to Shoreham meadows, close-by south of the railway, in 1925 - whilst the original airfield mellowed as farm pastures until the mid 1930s.

On 19 December 1939 the initial batch of Canadian troops arrived in the UK. Then on 25 February 1940 the first squadron of CAF pilots, crew and support personnel, docked at Liverpool as another World War embraced the British nation. Canada had just 4,000 airmen at the start of the war, a figure to dramatically grow as sky-high conflict drew into the 1940s.

No 242 Squadron was made-up largely of Canadian airmen, although a number of them had been lost during the fighting in France. No 1 Squadron CAF came to the mainland as a complete unit and became operational on 26 August. Of the 125,000 aircrew of the Bomber Command offensive there were 9,919 Canadian fatalities.

Simon Morgan, Stockbridge. May 2002.

ALLIED AND ENEMY AIRCRAFT OF THE FIRST WORLD WAR.

Opposite: Sopwith seaplane of 1913 with 100hp Anzani engine. (Gote House)

Below: Sopwith IBI 135hp in French Air Arm insignia. (Gote House)

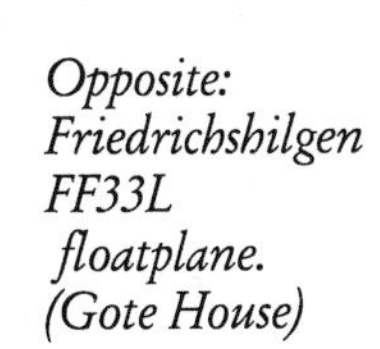

Opposite: Friedrichshilgen FF33L floatplane. (Gote House)

Below: Friedrichshafen FF31. (Gote House)

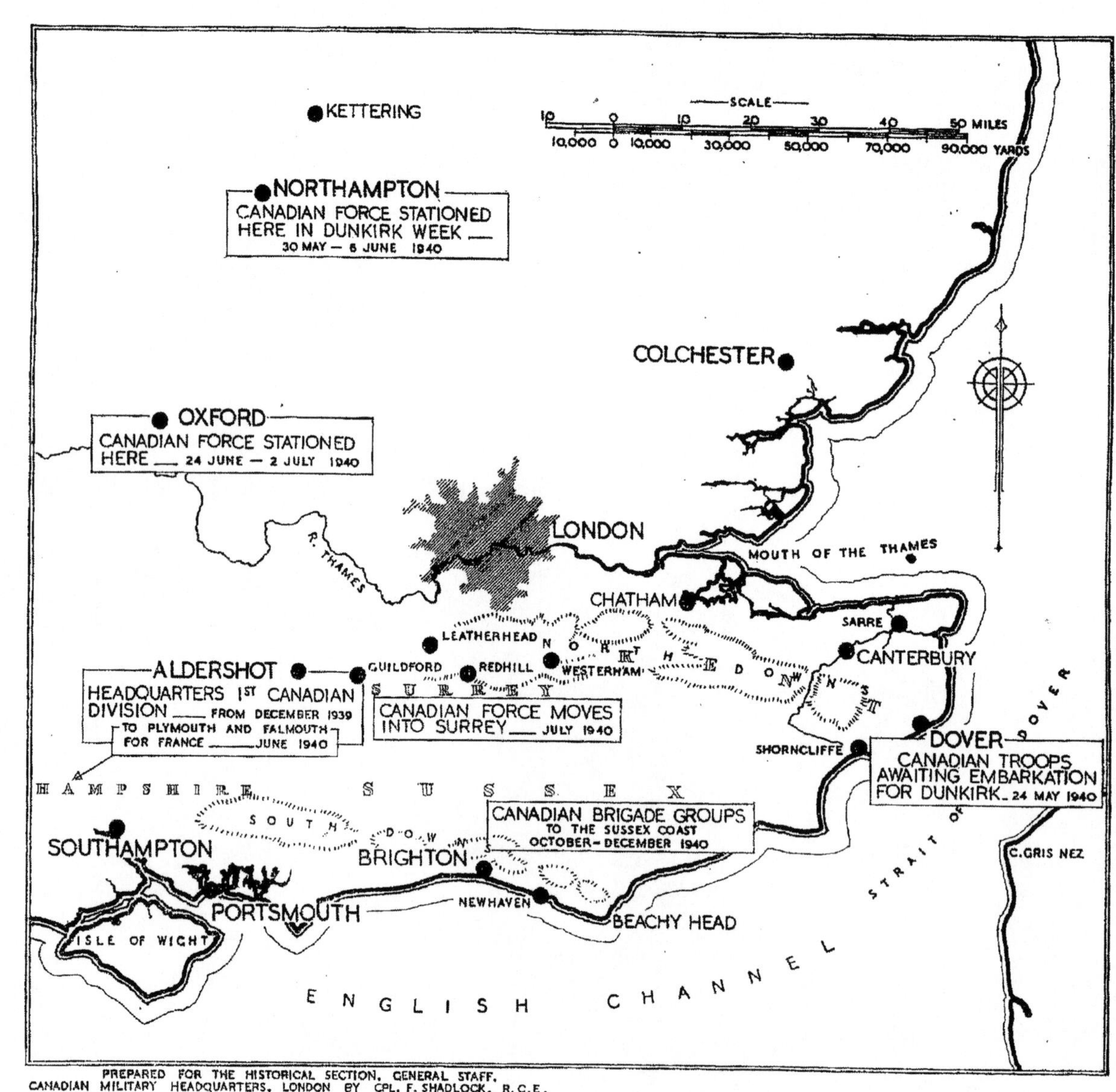

Canadian Military HQ, London.

THE SECOND WORLD WAR

SOUTH DOWNS TRAINING HAUNTS

I arrived in England 31 December 1939 with the Seaforth Highlanders of Canada, I was 20-years of age. The first few months we were in the Aldershot Command, then in various places such as Kettering and Wotton Park, then to Edenbridge in Kent. After a short stay there we moved to Oxted, Surrey.

Our first stay in Sussex was at the beginning of November 1940 when we moved to Brighton and were billeted with families. We only stayed a few weeks before returning to Oxted. There we remained for a year and then moved to Danny Park at Hurstpierpoint, near Hassocks, where we remained until August 1942. After training we always ended at a pub in Hurstpierpoint for a beer.

Our next move was a two-day march to Stone Cross, Eastbourne, via the coast road. On arrival in the Eastbourne area our Bren gun shot down two Focke Wulf 109s and the people of Eastbourne thought we were something special. We stayed there until April 1943.

On one occasion we stopped overnight just north of Seaford. At that time I was an Intelligence Sergeant and had been detailed to chose a suitable site for an overnight stay. I had just picked out an area when a local resident came up to me and said . . . Canadian Seaforth? That's where your lot stayed in the last war!

While we were at Danny Park I used to go every Sunday morning with Captain Simon Campion (whose family owned the Elizabethan Manor) and the local Home Guard units training across the Downs. I married a Land Army girl from Brighton and we have been married for fifty-nine years. *Intelligence Sergeant Maurice Phillips, Seaforth Highlanders.*
Point Clair QC, May 2002.

ENROLLED AT 15-YEARS OLD

I was at school in St Catherines, Ontario, during my early teens and I had never known my father to be in work. Life was certainly frugal at that time. I went to school one morning, phoned my mother at lunch time and joined the Canadian Army that afternoon - telling them I was 18-years old. The population there at that time was just 9,000 people, many families knew one another and I was not fooling anybody about my age. I still have eight brothers and sisters living in Canada.

All Canadian soldiers were volunteers, I joined a troop train to Vancouver where I spent three months training. My father was already in our Army by that time, but us youngsters were not allowed overseas until the age of 18-years arrived. So eventually I came to the UK, landing in Scotland and then to Hunstanton in Norfolk. We were marched to Crowborough in East Sussex and I was allocated to billets in Beacon Road opposite the golf club.

I met my wife Daphne in 1943 at a dance in Rotherfield and we were married the following year. I had little to return to Canada for after being discharged at Pippingford Park Rehabilitation Centre in 1945 and we happily settled into family life in this area since those days. I became involved with Canadian Veteran's Association (UK) and have served as Chairman of the National Executive. At one stage we had 20,000 UK members, but this has dwindled to about 1,500 people now.

Many war brides came in for a considerable culture shock when they arrived in Canada. Soldiers received double pay once they married and sometimes imaginative talk lured English girls into supposed marital bliss in Canada. Reality though often led to disaster, as life in rural Canada could be a considerable time-warp experience for naive English women.

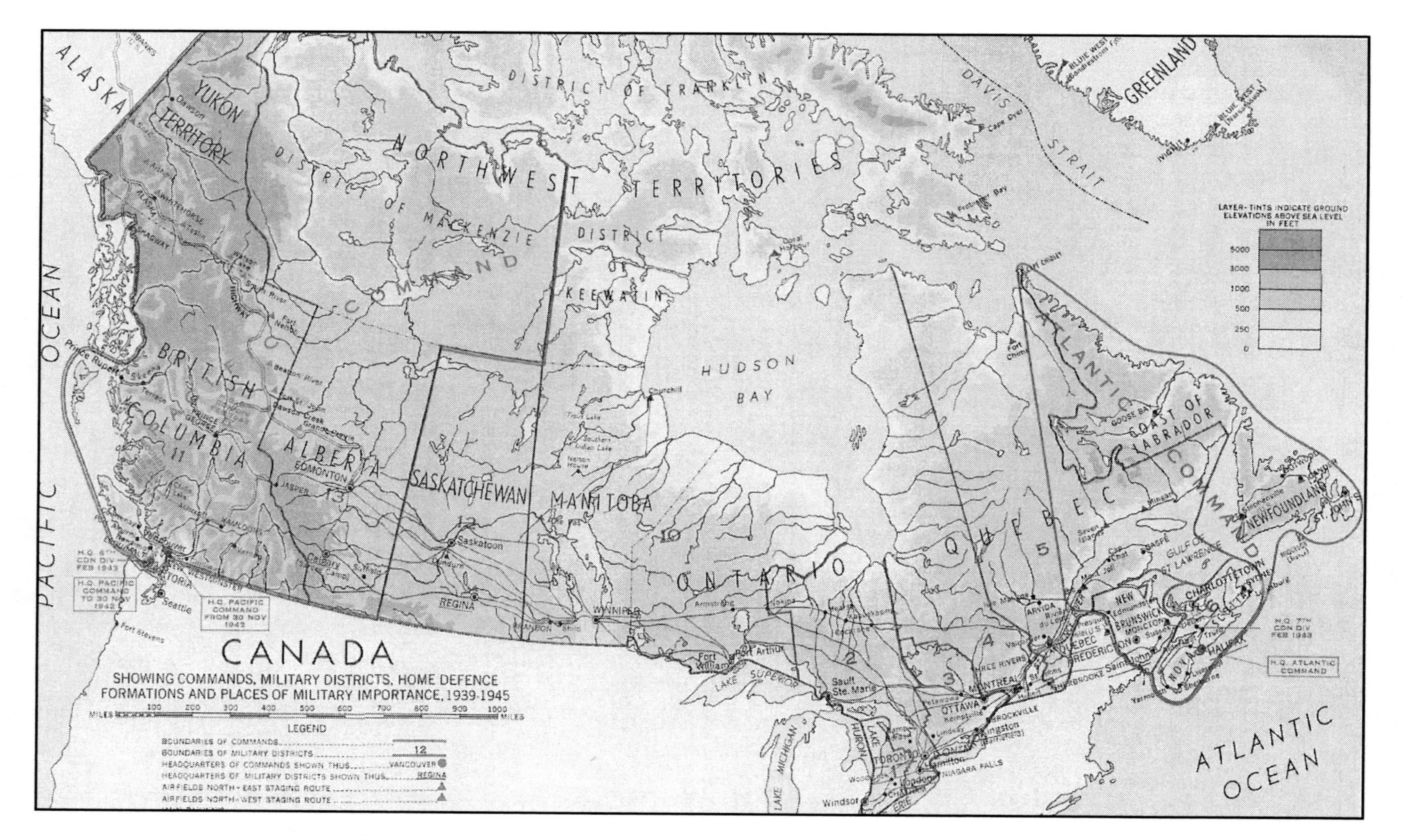

1940s CANADA. Showing Commands, Military Districts, Home Defence formations and places of military importance 1939-1945. (Canadian Defence HQ, Ottawa)

Some homesteads had no running water, power or sanitation laid on. A wood-stove might be in use, outside loos were literally common and generally primitive conditions prevailed in rural areas. Some women had married men of Indian descent with their traditional life-style, others found themselves living on remote farm plots in bleak conditions. Relationships at times failed for these reasons and in many such situations the Canadian Veteran's Association has been a welcome life-line for families in distress.

Bill Smith B40914, 4th Division, Lincoln and Welland Regiment.
Jarvis Brook, Crowborough. May 2002.

THE FRUSTRATING 1941-1942 PERIOD

Briefly in mid-1941 the 2nd Canadian Division exchanged locations with a British division guarding aspects of the Sussex coast. Then the Canadian Corps that autumn relinquished the role of GHQ Reserve and moved into the county.

Lt-General Bernard Montgomery opted to call his command the South Eastern Army and worked his troops, including the Canadians, hard. Starting with Exercise *Bumper* in late September 1941 when a dozen divisions battled their way across southern England. His Exercise *Tiger* followed in May 1942 and these exercises became known as legendary examples of rigorous training.

It is said though at this time the Canadian troop morale in Sussex was at its lowest ebb and that winter of 1941-1942 was noted as the coldest for some fifty years. Although good relations developed with our Home Guard units the 1st Division had been in England for about two years and the Canadians saw no suggestion of battle action. The volatile French-speaking Royal 22e Regiment, the Van Doos, particularly felt frustrated at their situation.

Robert Sanderson, Chichester. May 2002.

BOYHOOD BONDING AND TRAGEDY

My interest is solely with the 1st Battalion Argyll & Sutherland Highlanders of Canada (PL.). I was living at Uckfield during the war where my father was a serving Police Constable. He had fought in the Great War with the Coldstream Guards and was too old to serve in the Second World War.

The above Regiment arrived in Uckfield on 6 November 1943, leaving Tilbury on 16 and 18 July 1944. My interest was with the signallers based in a house on the south side of the Police Station, on the opposite side of the road. Before Christmas 1943 I was run over by a dispatch rider on the bridge in Uckfield High Street.The rider was called Lorne, he subsequently visited me in hospital and at my home frequently - we all became good friends. In order to identify him I wrote, in my retirement, to the authorities in Canada. In the September 1996 issue of *Albainn*, the Veterans magazine published in Hamilton, Ontario, there was an item identifying Lorne as Lance Corporal Lorne Marr B46286, Signals Platoon, killed in action at Igoville France on 27 August 1944.

I visited his grave in October 1996 in the Canadian War Cemetery at Calais. I have a copy of the Roll of Honour indicating that 267 men of that Battalion were killed. Photographs taken at Up Park Camp, Kingston, Jamaica, during the Battalion tour of duty between September 1941 and May 1943 identify nine soldiers. On a lighter note my father, as a former Guardsman, despaired at the casual manner of the Canadians. He warned Lorne as to the dangers of despatch riding, which as a sniper he claimed to have expert knowledge.

I recall my father assisting Canadian Engineers during 1940 preparing defence posts at two specific sites in Uckfield. These contained food and weaponry. In the event of invasion our family were to make for an identified fortified post.

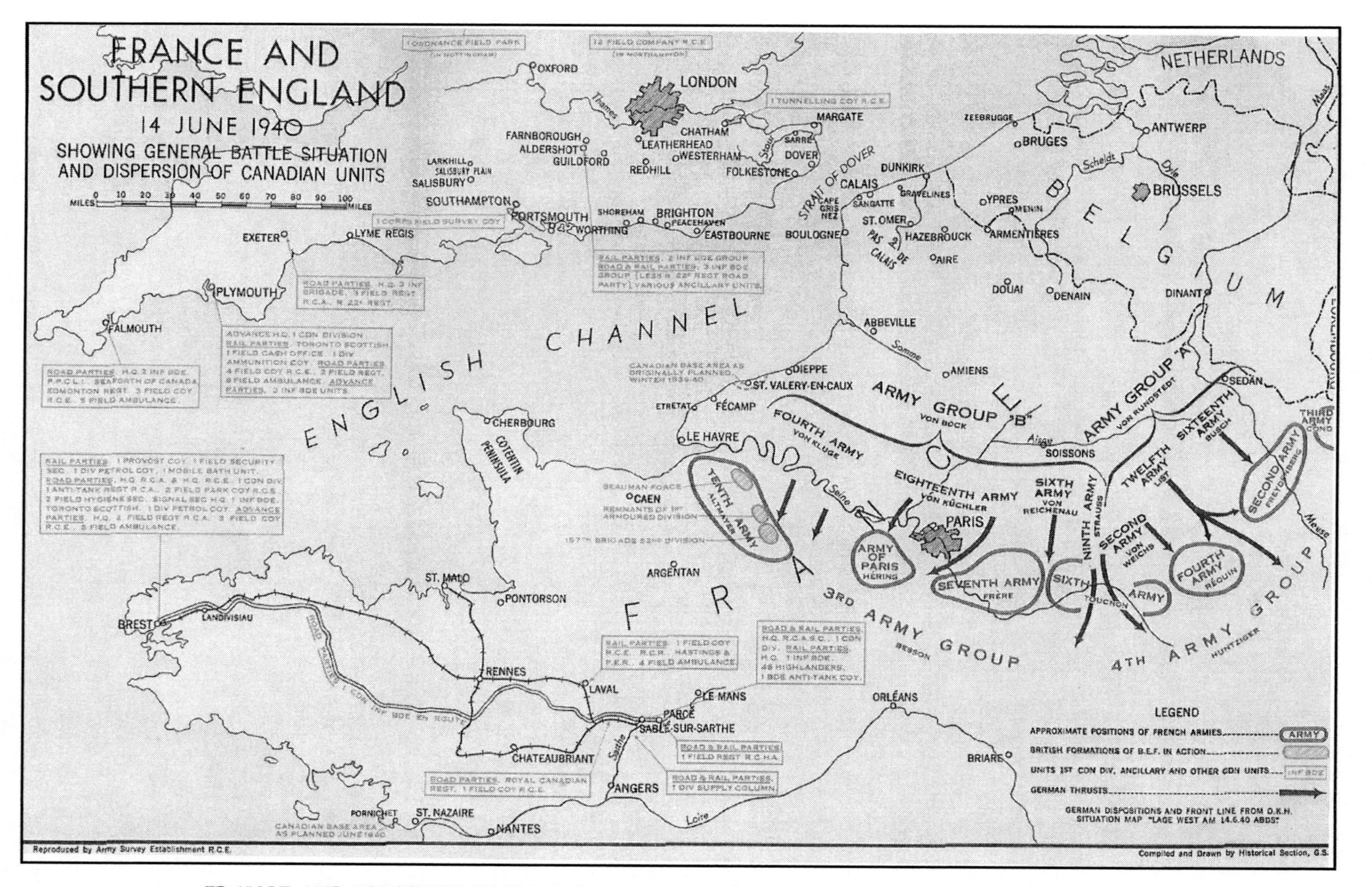

FRANCE AND SOUTHERN ENGLAND 14 June 1940. Showing general battle situation and dispersion of Canadian units.(Canadian Defence HQ, Ottawa)

Lorne Marr is seen with Peter Hunter, holding their cat, and his brother in Uckfield in 1944. (Peter Hunter)

The last resting place of Lorne Marr, at the Canadian War Cemetery in Calais. (Peter Hunter)

Daily the battalion Pipes and Drums beat the Retreat in early evening near Uckfield railway crossing in the High Street. They always played the Regimental march the *Campbells Are Coming* which was much enjoyed by the locals. The band wore kilts and tartan which added colour to a drab period. I recall the sad losses of July/August 1944 in the town.

Peter Hunter, East Grinstead. April 2002.

YOUTHFUL RECOLLECTIONS

The Canadians invited all the local children to a Christmas party at the Isle of Thorns camp at Chelwood Gate, near Crowborough, in 1943. We were given chocolate and many other wonderful things which were sent to the Canadians from home, every child received a present. Many Canadians smoked Sweet Chaporal cigarettes. We children used to collect the empty packets which had printed details of types of military aircraft - Allied, German and Japanese. We tried to be the first to collect a set of 50 cards. We certainly helped keep our village tidy!

One of the units stationed at Sheffield Park were the French Canadian Van Doos who very boisterous and all wore beards. I cannot forget them because during my National Service in 1952 in Korea I fought alongside the Van Doos - which was quite a coincidence.

There were countless Canadians stationed here before D-Day and many families in Danehill befriended them. They used to bring many 'goodies' sent from home which we did not have. One or two local girls married Canadians and went to live there after the war.

Before D-Day Canadian troops were stationed in the woods north of Springfield Cottage, there were large numbers there - right up to Forest Farm.

David Etherington, Danehill Parish Historical Society. May 1995.

From Warnham To D-Day

I was stationed in Warnham in the winter of 1943 with the 4th Canadian Armoured Troops Workshop, Royal Canadian Electrical and Mechanical Engineers. Our workshops were set up by the railway tracks in a brick works. We were billeted in woodland huts beside a large house where officers had quarters, our mess was in a large lean-to attached to the main house.

Horsham was the closest town to Warnham and we spent much time visiting the town for pubs, darts or talk with locals. Not all the townsfolk were amenable as Horsham was surrounded by military personnel and some of them did not behave as well as they should.

We moved to Guildford in the spring of 1944 for six weeks. I was an instructor for waterproofing Bren gun carriers for the D-Day operations. After this we moved back to Warnham where we had tents as the weather had improved a lot. I think it was around 8 June that one of the first flying bombs flew over Horsham and landed around Croydon.

When we left finally Warnham we went to London and then to the marshalling area awaiting orders for sailing. We left for France on a Russian ship called Samarovski as part of a convoy of thirty-three vessels. I was one of the first to go over the side and down the rope netting to an American landing craft, from there I went the rest of the way to shore on a British Bren gun carrier.

Raymond F. Milligan, Alberton, British Columbia, 1994.
(Horsham Museum, Horsham District Council)

Tales From Westfield Cricket field

As a twelve-year old lad during the war I lived in the village of Westfield, on the A28 about three miles from Hastings. We had Canadians staying there for a while, billeted in a large house called *Moorhurst*. It is now a specialised home, as you leave the village it is the last house on the left just past the football field.

I have no photos or letters, but I do remember that troops trained on our cricket pitch with guns and searchlights much to our delight, local people may confirm this as 1944. The pitch and original pavilion is still there. My story is they started me smoking, because we used to buy their cigarettes. Then when I arose one morning all the troops had left overnight and village life began to return to its pre-war pattern.

Bill Maylam, Westfield, Hastings. April 2002.

Family Life-style Shared

Your interest in Canadians stationed around Eastbourne during the war revived memories. When I was about ten or twelve we lived in Hurst Road with my mother and my grandparents. My father was in the navy on Russian convoys. In Mill Road, on the corner of Prideaux Road, there is a large house which is now four or five flats. During the war several Canadian officers were living there and my mother used to do the laundry of some of them. A corporal would bring their washing around for my mother to wash and iron.

It was also beneficial apart from the money which came in handy. We also got presents of things like a nice ham joint, chocolates and oranges. I remember the last Christmas we had before they left for the war. We had invited the corporal to share our Christmas dinner and he came with a bottle of whiskey for my grandfather and a huge box of chocolates for us. We had a grand time, shortly after, just before they all left to go to the war, my grandmother received a letter thanking the family for making him feel at home - that was the last time we saw him. Though after the war I believe we did receive a Christmas card from him.

D.J. Taylor, Eastbourne. April 2002.

LEWES IN 1942 RECALLED

Our family lived in the Old Naval Prison in North Street, Lewes. My father had served in the Royal Artillery for over twenty years, latterly as a Drill Instructor. On retirement from the Army he became the caretaker at the Old Naval Prison landmark in Lewes and as youngsters we loved playing in the haunting maze of rooms. There was a de-activated 6-inch gun for training in the yard, but this was removed early in World War Two.

Two regiments were billeted in there, until they were on the Dieppe Raid in 1942. These regiments were Fusiliers Mont-Royal and South Saskatchewans. There presence has become part of the county town's history, but today newcomers know little of those dark days in the early 1940s.

We awoke each day only able to anticipate what was happening along the coast and countryside. Life could have been so different today if the county had not been defended so vigorously.

Betty Kidgell, Lewes. April 2002.

Jesse Kidgell, Betty's brother, with their dog and a Canadian named Gerry.

HEATHFIELD AREA ASSOCIATIONS

Recollections of Canadian troops stationed around Possingworth Park, at Cross-in-Hand near Heathfield, remain clear in my mind. Soldiers of the Algonquin Regiment exercising with Bren gun carriers are recalled before they left in July 1944. Other troops from the Royal Regiment of Canada, the Toronto Scottish Regiment, and the Cape Breton Highlanders were stationed at Roy Hill Camp, Hadlow Down and The Wilderness near Heathfield. Relics of their activity remained for many years around the country-side - a variety of abandoned army vehicles and disposable equipment are now prized possessions in private collections. Recollections, or stories, from that period abound still as country people have a different pace of life to towns' folk. People around here can still visualise the time that Canadian soldiers became part of their life-style.

Members of the 1st Division Royal Canadians took over Five Ashes Garage on the A267 Tunbridge Wells to Mayfield road as workshop premises. I recall as a teenager the roads from Wych Cross to Crowborough being bordered by army huts, masses of them for miles over the Ashdown Forest, many of them had flower or vegetable patches outside, which all added to the seasonal colours of the heathland - providing troops with a productive pastime.

After my National Service in the late 1940s, mainly at RAF Rye, I worked for thirty-five years at the Kings Standing radio station near Crowborough. This massive bunker had been excavated in the early 1940s by a Canadian Army road building team to house the illicit Operation *Aspidistra* black propaganda broadcasts on enemy wave-lengths.

Ted Awcock, Cross-in-Hand, Heathfield. March 2002.

KEEPING IN CONTACT

Betty Fairbrass met Rowland Lecompete in the popular Regent dance hall in Brighton. Tragically the French Canadian corporal was killed shortly after arriving in France when the tank he was commanding was shelled. I have kept in touch with his sister and his two brothers.

Betty Fairbrass, Hove. April 2000.

Babies and Barns Distressed

I served in the British Army during the Second World War, but when on leave I often stayed with my sister at Steyning in West Sussex. There were a number of Canadian Army camps in that part of the county. Wiston House and Park nearby was a Canadian Battle School and they undertook training with live ammunition in the saucer of the Downs between Steyning Round Hill, Chanctonbury Hill and Cissbury Hill landmarks.

Soldiers, particularly from Wiston, would visit shops and frequent the many public houses around Steyning and Storrington. One day a party of Canadians in Steyning saw six or seven perambulators, complete with occupants parked outside Charlie Greig's grocers shop. The mothers were presumably inside queuing for their rations. As a lark the Canadians shuffled the babies around and put them into different prams. There was of course a terrible row about this and disciplinary action was taken. To this day, it is said, some Steyning families cannot be sure that they brought up the right child . . .

The Canadians field firing on the West Sussex Downs had to be accepted as part of the war effort, but it produced some sad results. Upper Maudlin farm, on the back of Steyning Round Hill, lost quite a lot of land which was included in the Canadian field firing area. This land included a very old barn with a medieval threshing floor. Unfortunately during exercises the barn was clobbered with 3-inch mortar bombs and became an unrecognisable ruin.

Sir Alan Leslie, Alfriston, East Sussex. July 2000.

Sioux Lookout Point!

Until mid 1998 I was resident in Hassocks, north of Brighton, and enjoyed the numerous footpaths of the area. One day I discovered an inscription on a remote railway bridge over the main London-Brighton railway line, known locally as *Mistys Bridge* between Lag Wood and Butchers Wood, south from Hassocks. The graffiti read PPCLI SIOUX LOOKOUT and an army serial number, PPCLI stands of course for the Princess Patricias Canadian Light Infantry. The wording was part way across the north side of the sandstone parapet.

I served in the Oxford and Bucks Light Infantry 1954-1956 - hence my knowledge of the PPCLI. I was for 21 years Woodland Supervisor at Wakehurst Place near Haywards Heath. The mansion and estate had been requisitioned for Canadian troops and I knew of several artefacts extant from that period.

Geoff Greenough, Sturminster Newton, Dorset. July 2002

Allies Home From Home

In October 1939 a contingent of Toronto Scottish soldiers were billeted in a girls' private school in Ditchling Road, Brighton. My parents gave several soldiers a 'home from home' during the war years. One of the Canadian soldiers was only 19-years old in the September of 1939 and he arrived in this country in October.

He was one of the 'boys' my parents welcomed. Neil married a girl from Eastbourne who went out to Canada as a war bride. Up until Neil's death in 1998 I have been in constant letter-writing contact and still write to his widow. My husband and I have visited Canada and met another of my parents' 'boys', Fred who was taken a prisoner of war at Dunkirk and taken in chains to a prison camp.

After the Canadians moved out of the school it was taken over by the Royal Artillery and then the Welsh Guards were billeted in house next to my parents. The night before they went to Dieppe they gave us a small sing-song to thank my parents. The top hat that went to Dieppe was given to them by my father. From just giving one lad a 'home from home' my parents gave a slice of home life to 43 nationalities . . . Canadian, American, Free French, Dutch, Polish and Australian.

Mrs S. Cozens, Brighton. April 2002.

Soldiers undergoing an obstacle course at the Battle Wing of the Canadian Training School near Worthing in June 1943. (Gote House)

Troops of the North Nova Scotia Higlanders exercise with Sherman tanks of the 27th Canadian Armoured Regiment (The Sherbrooke Fusiliers Regiment) at Wepham Downs, near Worthing. 14 April 1944. (Gote House)

TROOP ACTIVITY AROUND WORTHING

I will shortly be 65-years young and I remember outside our houses in Southfield Road, Worthing, were army trucks, tanks and equipment. I later found out that this division went over on D-Day and they suffered heavy casualties.

I believe this division also took over many hotels as billets in the Worthing area, including *Warnes Hotel* that was gutted by fire in the 1980s. I also recall that the Freemasons Centre in Upper Brighton Road, which was a Territorial Army drill hall when I was younger, was a HQ for a number of these Canadian units.

The main HQ for all Canadians stationed in Sussex was at Windlesham House School on the A24 north of Findon, Worthing. In 1940 it was used a base of petroleum warfare operations. The main training areas and rifle ranges in use at Kithurst Hill, off the Storrington to Amberley road, remained under Army control for many years and varied military relics remain on the countryside there.

Peter Knight, Sompting. April 2002.

INSIGNIA & TROOP MOVEMENTS

I am a life-long collector of British and Canadian head-dress insignia - cap badges. Regretfully, in a moment of madness, I sold my boyhood collection back in he mid-1950s, so I had to start all over again. I am sorry to say that there are a few that I have never replaced, mainly due to cost or scarcity.

During the war period, when the big build-up to D-Day was well under way, the area was choked with and Canadian troops. At that time (as a 15-year old) I compiled a list of Canadian units that I saw. The list consisted of four pages, written in pencil, out of a cheap writing pad. That list survived all these years and I still have it. It can be said that it is wholly genuine, in relation to the units named, as there were no books available listing such things and funnily enough the same situation exits today. It is still pretty well impossible to obtain a comprehensive book dealing with Canadian army badges. I have written to Canadian dealers with no result. The First World War insignia is available, but nothing emerges from the 1940s.

I know the Regiments, where they were stationed and the numerous country houses and institutions requisitioned and the camps. The Regiments in the main were Canadian Scottish, some French Canadian and even a tribe of North American Indians.

Les M.C. Brown, Uckfield. April 2002

(Note the Regimental Insignia section from page 111.)

The CVAUK Dieppe Day parade at Alexandra Park, Hastings, 1951. (Mrs F. Robinson)

FORMER HASTINGS CVAUK CHAIRMAN

My late husband, Tom Robinson, was stationed in various places in Sussex in 1940-1942 with the 14th Battery, 4th Field Regiment, Royal Canadian Artillery.

Tom returned to Canada in September 1942 on board the *Queen Elizabeth 1* (then a troopship) and was discharged from the Army as medically unfit in October 1942. After two years, and over 200 letters each, both ways, he was given permission to return to England in

September 1944. We were married in Hastings in January 1945. He joined the Hastings Branch of CVAUK (Canadian Veterans Association of the UK) and was their Chairman for some years until we moved away from Hastings.

The CVAUK held parades and reunions in various towns and held the Annual Dominion Day Service at Brookwood Cemetery, Woking, where many Canadian ex-Servicemen are buried. These include my husband's brother Harold who was killed in a road accident in Uckfield in November 1943 while he was stationed in Sussex with the Canadian Army.

Although Tom was discharged medically unfit in 1942 he lived until 1996 and was always proud to have served with the Canadian Army.

Mrs F. Robinson, Brigg, Lincs. April 2002.

EXTRACTS FROM TOM ROBINSON'S BOOK

June 1940. Arrived in Gourock, Scotland, then on to St Lucia Barracks at Borden in Hampshire. I had got my Machine Gunners badge so was posted to 14th Battery, 4th Field Regiment RCA. Then to Salamanca Barracks at Aldershot and later made a move to the south coast. We were billeted in a house called *Roughters* which I believe is still there at Icklesham.

As it was haying time I and another chap offered to help on a farm near Reading for two weeks. But our two weeks came to an abrupt end as we were recalled to move into Hastings to the *Robertson Hotel* on the seafront. (This was later bombed, but has been rebuilt). This was in September 1940 and we followed the Royal 22nds - the Vingt Deux of Montreal and some residents were surprised that we could speak English!

The town car park, opposite *The Robertson*, was then a gun park and we had to compete with the Home Guard for patrol duty. I was often on escort duty taking offenders to the glasshouse at Aldershot, or to the Royal Navy barracks at Chatham.

Manoeuvres took us to all sorts of places, like Larkhill near Stonehenge. In April 1942 we moved from Hastings to be under canvas, about ten miles inland. Then I was sent to Cove, near Farnborough, on a signals course where I was taken ill with pleurisy. While in hospital I heard of the Dieppe Raid on 19 August 1942, which is where I should have been, and where many of my mates were killed. But I returned to Canada and was discharged from the army.

Gunner Tom Robinson, M4174, 4th Field Regiment, RCA. 1972.

Tom Robinson likened the opportunity for a brew-up with colleagues in the bush to a picnic. Tom is seen centre wearing an army greatcoat. (Mrs F. Robinson)

WHO WAS THAT MAN?

Regarding the Canadian servicemen in Hastings during the war. My twin sister and I spent a happy time with them at a party for children who had relatives in Canada.

We had a sing song before the end of the party and I sat on a sergeant's lap and we sang *Kiss Me Goodnight Sergeant Major*. We are now 69-years old.

Miss E. Jones and Mrs P. Russell, Cranbrook, Kent. April 2002.

FLETCHING PARISH AT WAR

At the turn of the millennium the rural community of Fletching, a few miles west from Uckfield, might be remembered by a casual visitor for its busy High Street thoroughfare, its public houses and restaurants and rustic aura. Turn the clock back sixty odd years though and a rather vivid military influx was transforming village influences into the modern world.

Situated on the edge of the Ashdown Forest acres, that had witnessed a variety of army exercises since the Napoleonic period, Fletching received its first contingent of Canadian troops in October 1941. Le Regiment de la Chaudiere, a French-speaking Infantry Division raised in Quebec. Their camp was created in Sheffield Park, utilising the entrance that now serves the National Trust off the A275 Lewes Road.

Soon afterwards an adjacent camp was located in Sheffield Park. The 'Lewes Road' camp, above, plus 'Fletching' camp accessed via the Lodge archway from the village. In January 1942 the 4th and 105th Anti-Tank Batteries of the 3rd Canadian Anti-tank Regiment were the first to move into Fletching camp. By then familiar Nissen huts had been erected on concrete foundations amid a sea of mud, although there were no facilities like water, electricity, drainage, or roads until April that year.

A volume of hardcore for road construction at Sheffield Park is said to have come from bombed out sites in London. Camp life was barely durable and one soldier wrote home . . . How good the people of Fletching were to us. Private homes had local Women's Voluntary Service signs in their windows where a soldier could arrange to have a bath. They invariably left their soap, in rationed short supply to civilians, behind when they left refreshed. Another Canadian soldier noted . . . The publicans of Fletching, Piltdown and the *King's Head* deserve medals and wound stripes.

Sheffield Park House had become the Royal Canadian HQ by April 1942 with a NAAFI canteen and a YMCA recreations room. Brigadier Guy Simonds, who later commanded the 1st and 5th Canadian Divisions in Sicily and Italy, and the 2nd Canadian Corps from Normandy to Germany, was billeted in the *Sheffield Arms*. The Camp Commandant throughout was Brigadier Eric Snow. Both Le Regiment de la Chaudiere and the 3rd Anti-Tank Regiment, as part of the 3rd Canadian Infantry Division, were among the first to land on the D-Day Normandy beaches.

Also in April 1942 the Cape Breton Highlanders moved into Sheffield Park, replacing French Canadian contingents. The battalion also had one Company at *Searles*, where they stayed until the spring of 1943. At this time the 17th Field Regiment moved into the original Fletching village camp, until August that year - when they were replaced by the 5th Light Anti Tank Regiment RCA. A bronze plaque in St Andrew & St Mary the Virgin parish church at Fletching commemorates their presence.

This plaque is placed here by the
5th Canadian LAA Regiment RCA
in appreciation of the privilege of worshipping in this church.
August 1942 - March 1943.

One former member of that regiment recalls the occasion the camp was machine gunned by enemy aircraft. Certainly a variety of bombs were recorded as falling in the parish and several Allied fighters and bombers made forced-landings in the neighbourhood.

The Royal Canadian Army 8th Field Regiment arrived in Sheffield Park during February 1943, until July that year. In November 1943 further re-deployment of units took place within Sheffield Park. The 15th Field Regiment RCA, comprising 17th Battery from Winnipeg, 95th from Calgary and the 110th from Broadview were encamped with the 5th Anti Tank Regiment RCA whose Batteries were the 3rd Gananoque, 65th from Grenfell and the 96th from Edmonton.

It is recalled the 17th Battery were 'near the Lewes Road gate', the 95th and 110th 'along the shores of a little lake'. Officers were 'across the fence from the Manor House'. Both Regiments were part of the 4th Canadian Armoured Division of the 2nd Canadian Corps which fought from Normandy across to Germany.

The whole Division was assembled when they staged a parade on 17 May 1944 'on a Common near Forest Row'. The troops paraded before Canadian Prime Minister Mackenzie King. It is said the guard of honour led a drive past of tanks, artillery, half-tracks and trucks of all kinds, row upon row, eight abreast, followed by a Drumhead Service.

When the two Regiments left the Sheffield Park camps the terrain was used for training by Canadian Infantry reinforcements and finally the camps became Canadian repatriation depots in August and September 1945.

It is estimated that around 6,000 Canadian soldiers stayed in Fletching parish, at times, between October 1941 and September 1945. Alas, all too many of them never returned to their homeland.

Today little, if anything, remains to indicate the presence of Canadian troops within Sheffield Park. However, some older Fletching residents can still hear the echo of those Canadians brogues resonating across their village and surrounding meadows.

Adapted from a local project, courtesy of researcher Geoff Isted.

A War Bride's Experiences

By sheer chance WAAF Margaret Still (seen opposite in 1942) met Canadian Staff Sergeant William Finkle on a train at King's Cross station. She was on leave, on the way north with her mother to visit grandparents in Aberdeen. As the train was about to leave her brother, who was seeing them off, held the carriage door open and a pair of soldiers tumbled in. Railway carriages were single compartments in those days and soon the travellers began chatting avidly - which is the start of her own story . . .

Before we got off the train at Edinburgh Bill Finkle took my address. We went our separate ways, but arranged to met up again a few weeks later. Bill had told me he was an Ammunition Examiner, which I knew was a dangerous job. As our relationship developed Bill wanted me out of the forces. Then after our wedding we looked forward to the birth of our child - young Bill was born during an air raid at Camberwell in south London on 20 October 1943.

Our baby was just eight months old when the dreaded War Office telegram arrived. Bill and two other soldiers had been killed in an unexplained accident near Lewes, just ten days after the D-Day landings.

I remembered my promise that Bill had light-heartedly requested - to visit his parents in Canada if anything happened to him. Eventually the time came for us to visit Canada and my father and my brother escorted us to a departure venue in London. The place was full up with war brides going to live in Canada. Young Bill and I were put into coaches and taken to a railway station, arriving at Liverpool the next morning. We were helped onto the SS *Cavina*, where we shared a cabin with another girl who had a small daughter. We got on well, but my little boy was sea-sick for a few days. At last, after twelve days on board, we arrived at Halifax where there were more questions and forms to fill in.

The next episode was by train for five days to Edmonton, this was in very comfortable surroundings and the food was excellent. From Edmonton we travelled to the small town of Ponoka. My in-laws had a lovely home, but they were not used to having a young child around. We stayed nearly one year, but I was very home-sick and returned aboard the SS *Cavina* to England when the war finished.

I met some lovely people in Canada, with whom I still keep in touch. Later on I received a Canadian pension which to me is a miracle, I am so grateful.

Margaret Taylor, Worthing. April 2002.

The circumstances leading to the demise of Staff Sergeant William Albert Finkle, and two other soldiers in an accident near Lewes on 16 June 1944, were never fully revealed to his widow Margaret. Due to a series of mix-ups at the time she was unable to attend his funeral at Brookwood Military Cemetery.

(Margaret Taylor)

AT HOME IN HASSOCKS

We had the Queen's Own Rifles of Canada in Hassocks when I was a child during the war and my mother, the late Edna Williams, was involved in organising entertainment for the troops. She played both the piano and sang and was friendly with Vera Lynn who was also involved.

For years after (and during) the war my mother received a Christmas card simply addressed to . . . Edna, Hassocks, England, from the officers and men of the Queen's Own Rifles. Somehow the cards were all safely delivered!

At Christmas 1944 when I was six a Canadian officer gave me a magnifying glass in a red leather case, decorated round its rim with maple leaves and I still have it. Like many children I collected cigarette cards and although they were no longer made during the war, the Canadians smoked a brand called Sweet Caporal. Printed on the reverse of the packets were silhouettes of Allied aircraft - lots of different ones and I built up quite a collection.

My grandfather, Captain Pearson, was a retired army officer so virtually every night there would be a jeep or an army lorry packed in our drive at 41 Adastra Avenue, Hassocks. The HQ for the Queens Own Rifles was for a time in Scotland Cottage which faced on to the Recreation Ground at Hassocks just down the road from us. Nissen huts were occupied by the troops in the woods fronting London Road, known as the Canadian Woods.

Michael Worthington-Williams. Capel Iwan, Carmarthenshire. October 2002.

LEWES GARRISON TOWN

As an impressive 12-year old Lewes lad in 1940 John Tillstone grew-up with the threat of invasion as an almost daily aspect of life near the south coast. Enemy paratroops and sea-landings were anticipated at any time, before the tide of war turned to the Allies favour.

John and his boyhood friends could identify each aircraft by it's engine tones and the whole aura was one of excitement, not fear. On one occasion he recalls looking out of their front window at incoming aircraft, then dashing to the back of the house to see the planes go over. Dramatically a blast struck the front window of their Valence Road home, where John had been less than a minute previously. Enemy aircraft would appear low enough to see the aircrew faces, as they flew low over the county town.

On another occasion a rogue shell from Canadians, practising off Brighton racecourse or the Alfriston ranges, careered along Valence Road. Fortunately there was nobody about and MP's soon arrived, taking the shell away. Despite such intrusions John's mother would carry on scrubbing their front pavement and doorstep, or going about her daily routine. They only went to the ARP shelters twice and had no Morrison or Anderson shelters at home.

Many incidents concerning Canadian troops remain in John's mind. Of the more printable incidents as lads they were quite impressed how soldiers would pull a train emergency cord *ad lib* to alight where they liked and get to back to camp quickly. In February 1943 King George VI was scheduled to inspect troops of the Three Rivers Regiment, based in Worthing, who were assembled on the Downs. The parade waited, and dutifully waited, but in the cold weather the men needed to relieve themselves - although the officer in charge denied them such a convenience. Eventually the officer relented and the troops found a suitable ditch for their needs. Just at this time the royal party arrived and King George was noted giving a passing a grin at the spectacle of the troops dilemma.

The Calgary's were based in Seaford, the Ontario 1st Canadian Tank Brigade near Brighton with the French-Canadian Three Rivers Regiment at Worthing. As youngsters it was a familiar spectacle to see Canadian soldiers around Lewes. They manned Churchill tanks and Canadian-built Lee Ram tanks on exercises and often assembled in Spital Road near Lewes racecourse. The presence of Canadian soldiers remains vivid in many a youngsters memory from the time they grew-up in Sussex. John has made a study of Canadians in Sussex as an on-going pastime since the late 1940s and has contributed considerably to these archives. *John Tillstone, Lewes. April 2002.*

Doodlebug Disaster at Crowborough

Wednesday 5 July 1944 was a black day for Canadians camped on Crowborough Common golf course. The incident has been recalled by local resident Len Wickham who was a 12-year old lad at the time. His father was in the Home Guard, that occupied the golf links caddy's room below the sealed-off club-house and Len and his pals would play for hours across the gentle sloping countryside. Crowborough Home Guard took turns with Canadian soldiers to protect the 70-acre illicit King's Standing broadcasting station, its powerful 600-kilowatt music could be picked-up locally. A team of road construction Canadians had been involved excavating the secret counter-espionage station. Units worked over a 24-hours schedule daily and took three weeks to dig out the split level reinforced bunker for the Operation *Aspidistra* propaganda programmes that intercepted German domestic wave-lengths.

Many of the large houses around Crowborough had been requisitioned for troops, including *Brittany* and *Normands* in Southview and Beacon Road - plus nearby *Windlesham House* where the famous author Conan Doyle had lived. Postwar, as elsewhere, these once grand homes were in a poor condition, due to lack of maintenance and abuses, and many had to be re-built. Len recalls army exercises in the adjacent fields, the quarry assault course and training manoeuvres, where youngsters exchanged cordial banter with the Canadian troops.

Flying bombs usually descended when their motor cuts-out. Crowborough is situated high on the North Downs, 749-feet above sea level. Around 6.20pm on 5 July 1944 a doodlebug came in low and struck trees bordering the golf course, near High Broom Road.

In the ensuing mayhem it was found that seven soldiers had died and 19 men were seriously injured. This was one of the county's worst doodlebug incidents. The men belonged to the Lincoln and Welland Regiment. The incident is commemorated with a memorial in a spinney alongside the fairway. It is also perpetuated nearby off Fermor Way, in the road names Lincoln Way and Welland Close. A garden of remembrance has recently been established close to All Saints Parish Church at Canada Green off Church Road, Crowborough. *Len Wickham, Crowborough. April 2002.*

Cinderella's Story

My husband Captain Ken Mackenzie served with Royal Montreal Regiment and was stationed in Seaford town centre. They remained in Seaford longer than any other regiment and were well-known at the *Pelham Club* run by Rhoda and Sandy. I recall playing Cinderella in the only pantomime when we performed on the quay at Newhaven. Ken and I were married just before he left for *Juno* Beach landings in France during 1944. He was reported as dead, but was eventually taken to Douville Hospital. Ken always suffered with head injuries from this experience and he passed away in 1997. I came back to England after living in Canada all those years.

I served as Elizabeth Mackenzie and have since re-married and my name is Reeves. As Wren Elizabeth Slater I served on the telephones stationed in the Royal Navy unit HMS *Forward* tunnelled network at South Heighton between 1942-1945, until I was transferred to the former *London and Paris Hotel* at Newhaven that had been commandeered as a signals office. *Elizabeth Mackenzie. WRNS 54960. Rudgeley, Staffs. April 2002.*

ONE OF MANY

This story is similar to thousands of other stories, about young Canadian soldiers, volunteering their services to Great Britain at the start of the Second World War.

My name is Andre John Rivard and I am the wartime son of Private H16032 John alexander Rivard. Born: Voger, Manitoba, Canada 20 October 1920. Enlisted 7 September 1939 in Winnepeg. Regiment- Princess Patricia's Canadian Light Infantry.

My father's story, like so many others is about three years of reperticous inactivity, boredom, kept in damp Victorian barracks, antiquated bivouacs and tents, in and around south central Sussex. Churchill and the Canadian High Command for improving morale decided to let some Canadian soldiers go and billet with families in Brighton and Hove. My father billeted in the Kemp Town area of Brighton and met my mother at the Odeon Kemp Town. With a new change of life-style and a raised spirit they were married. I was born June 1943, three months after my father finally saw action. *Andre Rivard, Brighton. July 2002.*

EAST SUSSEX MEMORIES FROM EIRE

A military presence has been with us since the time my husband served as a Captain with the 23rd Field Regiment RCA. They were issued with self-propelled guns (SPs) mounted on Canadian-built Ram tanks.

The troops were billeted in Eastbourne from August 1943 to March 1944 when they transferred to Pippingford Park on the Ashdown Forest, prior to embarking for Normandy. The 23rd were in almost continuous action until VE Day in 1945. John was flown out to hospital after a tank accident on the road to Falaise in a crowded night attack.

Lance Bombardiers Gray, Drovin and Williams are seen in Darley Road, Eastbourne, eagerly waiting service from the NAAFI van. (Mrs Amy Monohan)

'Gunner Kenny' became the soldiers locally adopted mascot. (Mrs Amy Monahan)

The Protestant nuns of Notre Dame Convent, opposite the Pippingford Park billets, ran a war emergency hospital and used to pray for the troops whenever the regimental guns were moved out. The convoys went to Salisbury Plain or the Alfriston ranges, or up to Redesdale, for gunnery practice and the nuns presumed they were going to France each time. The convent made some large rooms available at Christmas 1943 for the other ranks Christmas dinner and social gathering.

Army drivers found the English villages and roads hard to manoeuvre through with their tanks and one time a gunner crashed a gate-post and pulled up just in time to peer out of his driving slit and come eye-to-eye with a surprised old lady looking out from her front window. He simply said . . . Good morning Mam.

On another occasion a driver crashed into a house in a small village. They told him . . . That house is 500 years old. He responded . . . Oh! I am so relieved, I thought was new, in Canada they are inclined to demolish old things in favour of new.

I lived in Canada for a couple of years and loved it there, we occasionally met ex-soldiers who had happy memories of their time in England. I am surprised how many of them settled in Sussex postwar. Though they used to say that in WWIII they need not send over any Canadian soldiers - just send their uniforms.

I came to England with the Canadian Red Cross. My husband John was a lawyer in Canada, but later moved to Eire to farm the family estate. We were married fifty-nine years ago in Toronto, my husband died in 1994 aged 82-years and I still have his letters from 1943 to 1945 written to me in Canada. He had taken his sons back to Sussex and Surrey. One daughter lives in Brighton and another daughter lives on the edge of Salisbury Plain. I have researched the history of this place back over 500 years and many wars. The castle was slighted by Cromwell and the steward hanged in the rebellion of 1798.

Mrs Amy Monahan, Castletown Castle, Carlow, Eire. May 2002.

A Land Army Girl At East Dean

Prior to the Dieppe Raid a company of the Canadian troops (I think they were the Cross Keys Division) were stationed in the *Birling Gap Hotel* near Seaford, with their Staff Sergeants in some of the bungalows such as *Gorsedown*.

As a Land Girl with a milk round we used to deliver to their cookhouse. Two of the Canadians, farming brothers named Ken and Robert from Saskatchewan, spent most of their leaves with my uncle and auntie at East Dean. After the war my then widowed aunt was given a lovely holiday in Saskatchewan and Alberta.

Some of the Canadians were billeted in Jevington and Wannock and they used to walk over to the dances we held at East Dean village hall. I particularly remember an enormous cowboy named Chuck who was very tanned and wore the kilt with great style. I think he was with the Princess Alice Regiment. He was a splendid dancer, but after the Dieppe Raid they never returned to the area.

About 1944 the downland dirt road to Birling Gap, from East Dean, was tarred and then got churned-up by Churchill tanks. The Allies had a firing range off Cornish Farm and they supposedly aimed at a moving target which ran along the foot of the position below Belle Tout lighthouse. They made a mess of Belle Tout strafing it with ricochets, but whether firing out to sea as the real target, Belle Tout always got in the way. This was after the owner Sir James Purves Stewart, the eminent brain specialist, had ceased to live in the old lighthouse. Later the Bofors gun crews at Crowlink were manned by soldiers of the Royal Artillery, as were the searchlight crews.

Mrs Kathleen Cater, Polegate. May 2002.

Canadian troops man a 40mm Bofors AA gun on Brighton seafront outside the Grand Hotel in March 1943. (Gote House).

Troops of the 1st Canadian Army Tank Brigade align for royal inspection on downland at Rottingdean in February 1943. (Gote House)

HM King George VI has his back to the camera man as he arrives to inspect troops of the Ontario 173rd Regiment at Rottingdean on 13 February 1943. The vehicle is a British-made Lloyd Carrier and the tanks are Churchill Mk IV. (PA 162754 Canadian Archives)

A number of Canadian soldiers married local girls and settled in the area. In the early 1950s some of them formed Epsom Lions base-ball team, with a home diamond in the Court Recreation Ground. I remember Ray Valleau, Eddie 'Red' Armstrong *(seen above)*, George Cameron and Cheechoo 'Joe' Sinclair.

Family and friends made up a keen supporters club, which raised funds for uniforms and equipment and hired a coach for away games. Opponents included the USAAF (Bushy Park), US Navy (London), Kodak (Ilford), the Indians (Wellingborough), the Blue Jays and other Surrey sides. Leatherhead Maple Leafs, meeting at Randalls Park, were formed later with some of these players. *Patricia Hennessy, Epsom. July 2002.*

A STORY OF COINCIDENCE(S)

Joyce Brewer has told us the story of her life as a Hastings teenager in the Second World War. During her account she mentioned a Canadian soldier, Doug Powell, who was with the crew of the AA gun sited near her home in Broomgrove Road in 1942.

Doug was 19-years old in 1942 and must have cut an attractive figure, as he bore a resemblance to the then famous cowboy star Roy Rogers. Like him Doug had a pleasant singing voice. Joyce's family befriended Doug and he used to spend a lot of time with them, she and her family thought he was terrific.

His gun crew were not in Hastings for very long and they moved on. Joyce and her sister Hilda sent letters to him until he was shipped out to Italy. Then all the correspondence ceased. The family often spoke of him and wondered if he survived the war. Years passed, Joyce's brother and sisters were married, her Dad died and she remained at home with Mum.

After the war Joyce's Mum enjoyed playing bingo on Hastings pier, where she loved meeting people. One night a girl hurried in and on hearing her voice Mrs Brewer recognised her as a Canadian. Unaware of the vastness of Canada she told the girl about Doug Powell and she asked Mrs Brewer for his home town - Springhill, Nova Scotia. Astonished the girl said it was her home town and on hearing Doug's details she said she knew his family.

A year passed and the girl came once again to the bingo hall, where she told Mrs Brewer she had not forgotten the story and in fact was returning to Canada with her English boyfriend - who proved to be the brother of Joyce's friend Joan. Later Joan went to Canada to visit her brother and she took along Doug's details. Joan traced him and found that he was married and living in Fredericton, New Brunswick. Mrs Brewer wrote to Doug at once and he was amazed to receive the letter after so many years. In his reply he said that he had been in the Regular Army for 26 years and he and his wife Betty had five sons. Letters were exchanged for two years, then quite suddenly Doug passed away aged sixty.

Correspondence continued, but by 1986 Mrs Brewer was aged 84 and in poor health. Then an unexpected phone call came from Doug's widow and she was at Hastings station! She was visiting family and places in Britain with her son and wife and they decided to pay a flying visit to Hastings. They could stay only an hour, but they chatted avidly and were shown the site where Doug's Bofors had stood, taking photos also of Joyce and her mother.

Three weeks later Joyce's mother died. Joyce was glad they managed to trace Doug Powell after all those years and that they met some of his family. It brought her mother so much happiness - the result of an amazing coincidence. Joyce still corresponds with Betty.

Extracts from JOYCE BREWER'S WAR, Hastings.UK. net.
From *Victoria Seymour, Hastings.*

EXERCISES ON THE ASHDOWN FOREST

Many of the accounts now archived in this edition came about by chance meetings. One such occasion developed during a mid-1990s holiday when a contributor to the *Ashdown Forest News* met with Douglas van Kleek, who in 1943 served as a Captain with the 1st Canadian Mechanical Equipment Company in England.

He had been instructed to establish a school for British Army officers and service NCOs, in groups of six to eight men, to operate and use heavy mechanical plant, such as shovels, graders and bulldozers. The training was to later enable them to construct temporary AA gun emplacements and landing strips in Europe, courses lasted about a fortnight. The gun sites were levelled after each class, but the runway was extended class by class.

Captain van Kleek's recollection was of a cluster of timber buildings off the A26 highway, used previously by cyclists and walkers and these huts were taken over for mess rooms and administration as military operations. By July 1943 the British Army had taken over the site and the Canadians were moved under canvas. They closed down their classes by mid-September and moved across to Italy in October.

Thus the earthworks project terminated, although the heathland air-strip was used on several occasions for emergency landings in the mid-1940s. The site is known locally as The Old Airstrip and acknowledged by modern day light aircraft crews as an emergency landing ground. The earthen runway clearing is situated tangent west off the A22 between Chelwood Vachery and Ashdown Forest Farm and runs westerly towards the former Isle of Thorns boys camp.

Adapted from ASHDOWN FOREST NEWS. *Spring 1994.*

SERVICE AND SOCIALISING AROUND HORSHAM

We noticed your request in the *Vancouver Sun* for recollections. I served in the Horsham area for over six years, including time in Sicily and Italy. We were married at All Saints church, Roffey, in 1945. My wife's sister also married a soldier with the Canadian Scottish Regiment.

I was with 21 Battery, 6th Field Regiment, RCA and served several times at Denne Park where I guess we helped deplete the deer stock. Also where on finding a storage area under the main lodge we helped deplete the wine cellar. We spent many days building roads in Denne Park to carry our field guns and vehicles - the Buicks being trucked down from the bombed-out London areas.

We were also stationed at Petworth, Pulborough and Partridge Green. Many leisure hours were spent at YMCA hostels like those in Albion Terrace, Horsham, and the YMCA canteen upstairs in the Chart & Lawrence building. We also spent many hours at dances in the Drill Hall and a small dance hall on Hurst Road.

We have visited Horsham several times since the war, but found so many changes that we sometimes got lost looking for a certain place. My wife has kept in touch with many Horsham girls who are now living in Canada.

Whilst in Horsham my favourite watering holes were the *Hurst Arms* and the *Kings Head*, where we had some great sing-alongs etc. I believe all of the boys would say they were well-treated and received by the people of Sussex.

Jean and Wally McLean, New Westminster, British Columbia. 1994.

(Horsham Museum, Horsham District Council)

THE CANADIAN ARMY IN EASTBOURNE

Eastbourne turned out to be a beautiful seaside town nestled behind the great promontory of Beachy Head. Great hotels lined the broadwalk of Grand Parade which ran for several miles along the seafront. Most of them were closed due to damage from air attacks, and others were used as billets for the army and WAAF personnel stationed nearby. A large part of the civilian population had been evacuated and it was into their homes on the resort's western fringes at Meads that the 23rd Field Regiment RCA moved.

The only other Canadian unit in Eastbourne at the time was the 6th LAA Regiment. At a later date the 8th and 19th Field Regiments moved in, along with some 5th Division infantry, but they stayed only a few months. The 23rd was without equipment when it reached Eastbourne, so that the first six weeks were devoted to brushing up basic training subjects, foot drill, route marches and general hardening up. The South Downs bordering the town provided excellent material for any hardening activities, for simply to climb from the street beside Roger or Queen batteries to the top of the Downs was enough to ruin most men. It seemed to us that one could not go anywhere in Eastbourne without having to climb at least one good-sized hill.

A regular weekly feature for each troop was a bath and swim parade at the public Devonshire Baths on the seafront. For sixpence you could have a private bath and then swim in the pool wearing a moth-eaten Gay Nineties bathing suit which cost another few pence. Shortly after the regiment got to Eastbourne Major R.E. Hogarth arrived to take over the appointment of second in charge and Major Skaith took over the 36th whose BC, Major Chipeswick, did not come overseas with the unit. Within five days of arriving in Eastbourne the first group of men were away on privilege leave, with Scotland apparently a popular destination.

The surrounding downland provided ample scope for destructive shoots. The favourite target was named *Toronto Corne*r, a huge dew pond on the side of a ridge about 400-yards from the OP. Lt Pinkerton made a name for himself one day by dropping his first ranging round plonk into the crater.

As predicted in Canada the old question of 'What's in a name' stirred-up to trouble for the Regiment once more. The Army finally made up its mind that it took a dim view of the 23rd bearing the proud designation RCHA and finally on 3 November a quiet order went out from RHQ to the effect that RCHA shoulder flashes would be removed and officers would cease wearing ball buttons. In a week or so the Regiment was back to wearing its 23RCA flashed and very happy about the whole thing.

There was plenty of entertainment for everybody. Down town there were about five cinemas and dances were held nightly in the *Winter Garden*, a popular spot for the gunners of an evening. A bus left Meads every twenty minutes and reached the station down town in ten minutes. There you could catch a bus to Old Town where many a lad met many a gal. The families of Eastbourne were very friendly to the 23rd and many of the men found a home from home where they could drop in and be one of the family.

Batteries had their favourite pubs, such as *The Ship* where the 31st held forth and *The Pilot* which was practically a second home for the 83rd. Any night of the week you would find *The Pilot* crowded with 83rd lads drinking a few mild and bitters, talking about the present and the past and listening to the music which Bdr Stan Watkins poured forth from the corner piano. The *Beachy Head Hotel* was another popular haunt of our troops. A weekly regimental newspaper started during the fall, but it only lasted a few months. This was a four page mimeographed sheet christened *Ess-Pee* as the result of a name contest.

The Regiment paraded regularly to All Saints church in Eastbourne town centre for Sunday services. Captain R.L. Bacon, our padre, had been unable to come overseas with us, so we shared padres with the 6th LAA until Captain Bacon rejoined the unit. The Regimental band formed up on Sunday morning in Chesterfield Road and paraded to church about 20 minutes away. On Saturday mornings, following a battle-order inspection, the band usually led the Regiment on a route march out around the golf-course or through the town.

Another regular feature of training which evoked a lot of interest was the anti-tank shooting carried out almost weekly on the Belle Tout cliff-top ranges near Beachy Head. Two wood and burlap tanks used to run along a runway at varying speeds, looking fairly large, but actually not too easy to hit. The AP shoot would slice a hole through the burlap, or miss completely, and then ricochet up into the battered old lighthouse (Belle Tout) behind the range or else careen crazily out to splash in the English Channel.

Adapted from the REGIMENTAL HISTORY OF THE 23RD FIELD REGIMENT RCA,
courtesy of Mrs Amy Monahan, Castletown Castle, Carlow, Eire.

The battered shell of Belle Tout lighthouse near Beachy Head in 1946. The 1840s granite landmark unfortunately lay beside a bustling moving target tank range. See final paragraph above. (T.R. Beckett Ltd)

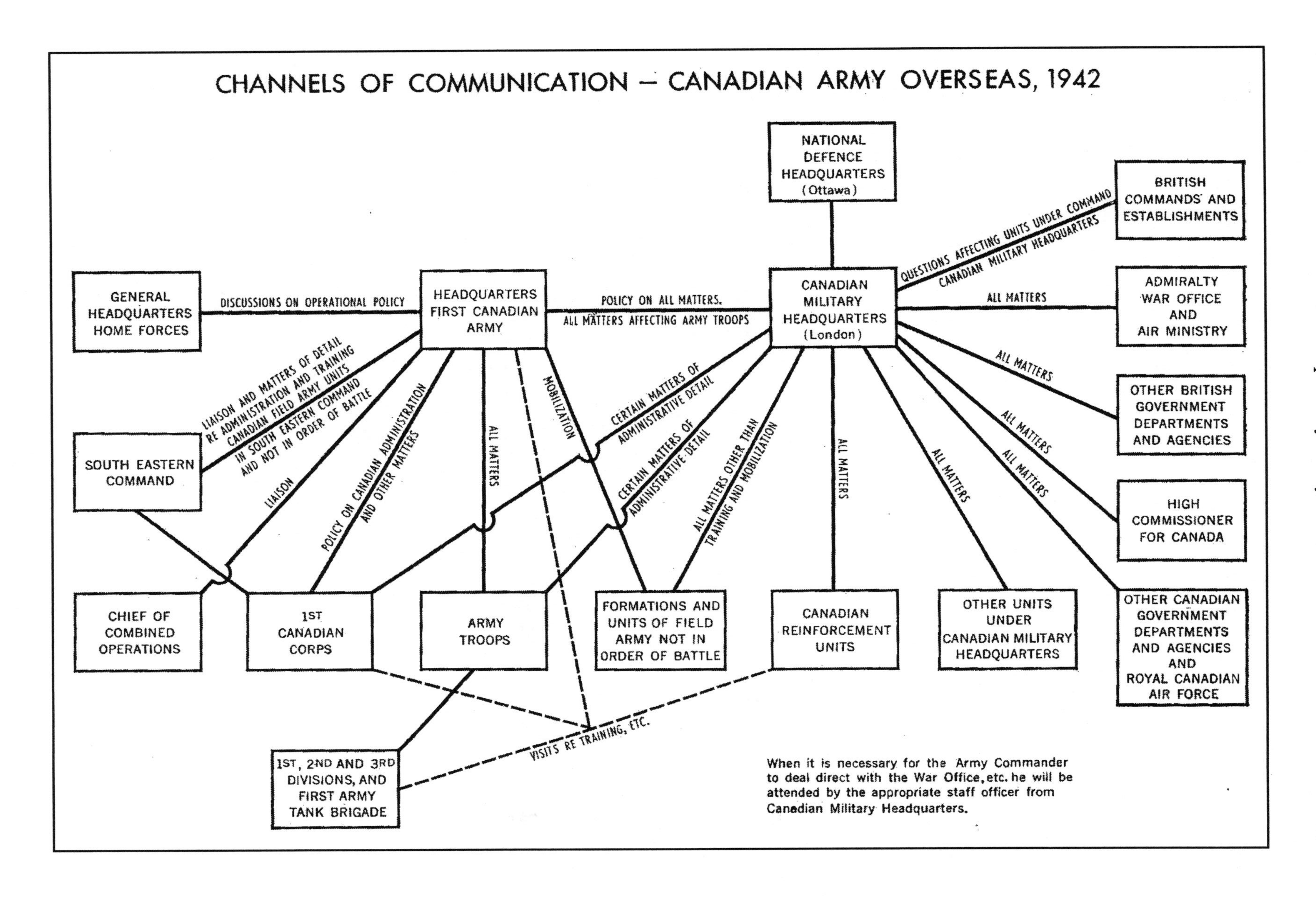
CHANNELS OF COMMUNICATION – CANADIAN ARMY OVERSEAS, 1942
NATIONAL DEFENCE HEADQUARTERS (Ottawa)
BRITISH COMMANDS AND ESTABLISHMENTS
QUESTIONS AFFECTING UNITS UNDER COMMAND CANADIAN MILITARY HEADQUARTERS
GENERAL HEADQUARTERS HOME FORCES
DISCUSSIONS ON OPERATIONAL POLICY
HEADQUARTERS FIRST CANADIAN ARMY
POLICY ON ALL MATTERS.
ALL MATTERS AFFECTING ARMY TROOPS
CANADIAN MILITARY HEADQUARTERS (London)
ALL MATTERS
ADMIRALTY WAR OFFICE AND AIR MINISTRY
ALL MATTERS
OTHER BRITISH GOVERNMENT DEPARTMENTS AND AGENCIES
LIAISON AND MATTERS OF DETAIL RE ADMINISTRATION AND TRAINING CANADIAN FIELD ARMY UNITS IN SOUTH EASTERN COMMAND AND NOT IN ORDER OF BATTLE
POLICY ON CANADIAN ADMINISTRATION AND OTHER MATTERS
ALL MATTERS
MOBILIZATION
CERTAIN MATTERS OF ADMINISTRATIVE DETAIL
CERTAIN MATTERS OF ADMINISTRATIVE DETAIL
ALL MATTERS OTHER THAN TRAINING AND MOBILIZATION
ALL MATTERS
ALL MATTERS
ALL MATTERS
ALL MATTERS
SOUTH EASTERN COMMAND
LIAISON
HIGH COMMISSIONER FOR CANADA
CHIEF OF COMBINED OPERATIONS
1ST CANADIAN CORPS
ARMY TROOPS
FORMATIONS AND UNITS OF FIELD ARMY NOT IN ORDER OF BATTLE
CANADIAN REINFORCEMENT UNITS
OTHER UNITS UNDER CANADIAN MILITARY HEADQUARTERS
OTHER CANADIAN GOVERNMENT DEPARTMENTS AND AGENCIES AND ROYAL CANADIAN AIR FORCE
VISITS RE TRAINING, ETC.
1ST, 2ND AND 3RD DIVISIONS, AND FIRST ARMY TANK BRIGADE
When it is necessary for the Army Commander to deal direct with the War Office, etc. he will be attended by the appropriate staff officer from Canadian Military Headquarters.

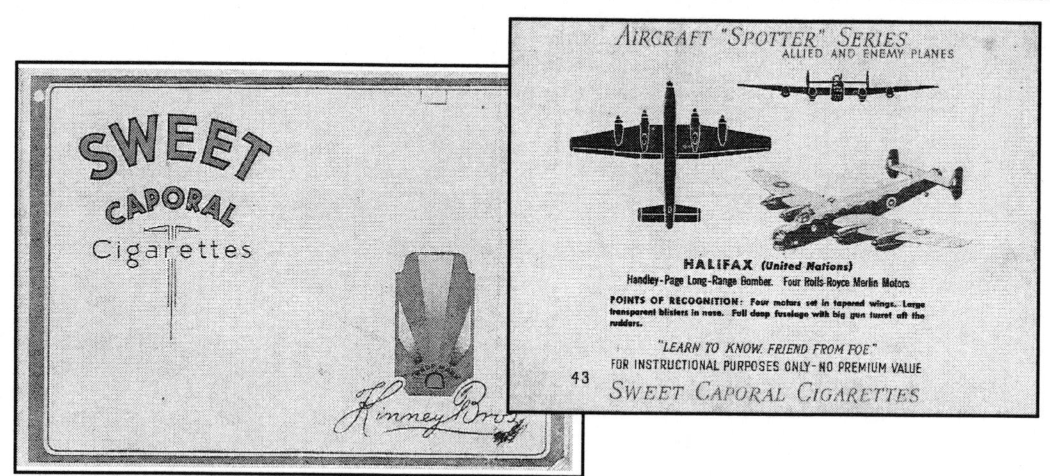

H.M.S. "REPULSE"

OVERSEAS

$1.00 SENDS 300

"BRITISH CONSOLS", "EXPORT", "MACDONALD'S MENTHOL", "SCOTCH BLENDS" or "LEGION" Cigarettes

or 1 lb. Tobacco—BRIER SMOKING or any MACDONALD'S FINE CUTS (with papers) also DAILY MAIL CIGARETTE TOBACCO Postpaid to Soldiers in CANADIAN ARMY OVERSEAS and to CANADIANS IN UNITED KINGDOM FORCES.

$2.50 SENDS 1,000 Cigarettes

Mail Order and Remittance to:—

OVERSEAS DEPARTMENT

W. C. MACDONALD INC.,

Box 1929, Place d'Armes, Montreal, Canada

This offer subject to any change in Government Regulations

SEND THE BOYS THE BEST

Collecting cigarette packaging for military information was one of our boyhood pastimes in the early 1940s. Cards would be swapped and pasted in albums as wartime activity was all around us. This hobby added considerable excitement to an otherwise drab and frugal period of time.
(Ted Awcock)

A despatch rider and locals stand by as Churchill MkIV tank, No 8 of B Squadron, ploughs ahead during Exercise Spartan - en route towards Oxford in March 1943. Somebody will be able to identify the location by that church. (Imperial War Museum H27928)

WEST SUSSEX POSTINGS

My outfit was the 34th Battery, 14th Canadian Field Regiment, RCA and for me part of 1942 was spent under canvas at Denne Park, Horsham. I can well recall the big rats running over us in the large MT tents as soon as lights went out. We moved to Summers Place, Billingshurst, in October 1942 and stayed there until December that year. The camp was mainly Nissen huts, although we spent little time in camp. We were inevitably on the move, relieving a regiment in the invasion area or going to the firing ranges in Wales.

From 13 March 1943 to September 1943 we stayed in a Nissen hutted camp at Five Oaks. This was very pleasant pastoral setting, it had its own sewage works, water system and ablution huts. My friend and I spent slow Saturday afternoons by dropping Thunder Flashes down chimneys at some huts or floating burning paper down the sewer main when the WO's were using it. Needless to day they soon changed the seating arrangements in the ablution huts. Some evenings and weekends were spent on a nice walk to the *Blue Ship* pub at Bucks Green. Tuesday was stock day for *Younger's Scotch Ale* at the *Kings Arms* in Horsham and one had to get there early to get any as it never seemed to last long.

My regiment spent most of its time in England around Sussex and Surrey, then in September 1943 we moved to Christchurch in preparation for D-Day. I enjoyed my stay in beautiful England, my A troop of the 34th Battery came from the small town of Gananoque and there are still some of us left to talk over the times as though they happened yesterday.

It always amazed me that a country the size of England could perform such prodigious feats. Where was the room found for the airfields, the millions of troops. And the industrial effort was fantastic. The railroads were the best - it is a wonder the whole system did not collapse under the strain. I can never remember a train being late when I was going on leave.

Robert J. Harper, Gananoque, Ontario, 1994.

(Horsham Museum, Horsham District Council)

MEMORIES OF HASTINGS

I am a native of Hastings and several Canadian units were stationed in the area area preceding D-Day, I would have been eleven or twelve years old at the time. The only unit that I was familiar with was stationed very close to my home in the Hollington area, in a large old house in its own grounds called *Brookwood* on the Saddlescombe Road. The unit was one of the Royal Hamilton Light Infantry (RHLI) which they themselves nicknamed the *Royal Hindu Lancers of India*!

Being fairly familiar I thought with British service discipline, my father was a Royal Engineers sergeant, I could not fail to notice the light-hearted and seemingly casual manner the Canadians went about their soldiering. Despite appearing well-turned out in public they were casual even when on duty. They fraternised freely with locals, including us lads and I recall that we were particularly quizzed about the availability of local females.

I distinctly remember when speaking with one sentry his crude comments - that are unprintable here. That sentry incidentally, apart from gassing away to all and sundry in common with his colleagues so engaged, sat in a chair at the vehicle entrance to *Brookwood* in Upper Glen Road!

This unit was equipped with Bren gun carriers and no restrictions seemed to be put on their usage. For example for local shopping trips and even rides and rudimentary mechanical instruction, plus weapons training for us boys. The regiment contributed several carriers and personnel to a local War Weapons Week procession, organised through my nearby private school - *Bal Edmund* now alas gone.

Only one member of the RHLI remains in memory and only because he married a local girl who was in the Women's Land Army and was a ringer for the film star Alexis Smith. I regret that I cannot recall his name, but on demob he joined the old Hastings Borough Police Force and presumably served his time and would be traceable. As we were later bombed out by a V1 my mother and I became camp followers of a sort and did not re-settle in the area for some period of time.

Keith Shoesmith, East Grinstead. May 2002.

Men of the Canadian 1st Division arrive in Scotland in 17 December 1939. (Canadian Army Archives).

The Churchill MkIII tank is distinctive for it's welded turret - here cables hold equipment steady during transit. (Imperial War Museum H27925)

GENEROSITY AND COMPANIONSHIP

In 1942 for two years I worked in the Land Army at Balcombe, near Haywards Heath, and had some very happy times with the Canadians.

They were a lovely bunch of guys, very kind and well-mannered, I enjoyed dancing at the Victory Hall with them and was entertained at Highleigh Manor, a lovely old house where they were billeted. They were very generous with their cigarettes and candies as they called them. My cousin married one from Hailsham, but sadly he was killed on D-Day.

I am aged 87-years now and often wonder how many of my old friends are still alive.

May Northcote, Hurstpierpoint. May 2002.

FIRLE VILLAGE COMMANDEERED

As a member of Firle Home Guard unit in the early 1940s I was taken aside one day by an officer and approached if I wished to be considered for special duties. So began my transformation from working as a horticulturist on the Firle estate to becoming patrol leader of *Badger II* unit No 203 battalion Home Guard, engaged on subversive rearguard duties in case of invasion. Our patrol consisted of six men and we worked from a sunken Nissen hut on the Downs overlooking Firle Plantation. Regular soldiers would supply us with food, left in a nearby dug out, for us to collect. I recall on more than one occasion we lost our issue of rum and Canadians camped nearby would get the blame for this loss.

Hereditary landowner Lord Gage in his account *Memories of Firle* says . . . The 1st Canadian Division had more than the usual percentage of doubtful characters. The worst example of their behaviour was when they broke into the cellar and drank all my wine. I remember I had several dozen excellent vintage White Burgundy, which I was told they drank laced with gin. The 3rd Canadian Division that succeeded them produced some of the finest men I have ever seen, alas they suffered appaling casualties in the Dieppe Raid.

One may draw one's own opinion on such appraisals. Certainly Firle parkland, along with numerous other estates, was occupied by exuberant young men, trained and keyed -up to fight for their motherland. Tensions built-up everywhere and nominal social intrusions became part of the daily Sussex life-style of the early war years.

The feudal format village of Firle became virtually a community under siege as Canadian soldiers and equipment dominated the area.

PLT. In memory of my colleague Bill Webber who Passed On - March 2001.

FROM SUSSEX TO D-DAY *Juno* BEACH

I served with the Canadian Army from July 1940 until I was demobbed in this country in September 1945, having come to England with the 13th Canadian Field Regiment RCA which was the 3rd Division arriving in Gourock, Scotland on 13 November 1941. We came down to Farnborough by train where we were issued with 25-pounder guns. We moved to Haywards Heath on 1 December 1941 and some of the Regiment were stationed at Lindfield. We stayed there until April 1941 and from there we did a lot of schemes and training, especially at the firing camp at Sennybridge in Wales.

From Haywards Heath at the end of April 1942 we moved to Denne Park in Horsham, where we replaced the 2nd Infantry Division which had gone to the Isle of Wight to commence training for the Dieppe assault. In May we went on Exercise *Tiger* which lasted twelve rain soaked days. There we were under the command of Lt-General McNaughton. In June 1942 we had a firing practice camp at Lark Hill, after which we moved to Wilmington - with some of the Regiment going to Firle Park and some to Seaford.

The next move was to Findon in August, then we spent ten days carrying out intensive training at Builth Wells. Then came a short stay in Worthing, with some of the Regiment at Brighton and Steyning. In December 1942 the whole Regiment moved to Billingshurst until October 1943. While we were there a German Dornier plane swept down and machine gunned the entire camp - not one man was injured.

In June 1943 I married a girl from Ardingly that I had met whilst stationed at Haywards Heath. From here short trips were made to the Alfriston ranges, leading up to the famous Operation *Spartan*. For this exercise General McNaughton took command of four Canadian divisions, which he pushed the opposition through southern England and into the Midlands. This exercise took twelve days and compo rations were issued.

In September 1943 came the first indications that the 3rd Canadian Division had been chosen for the initial assault on the Continent. The 13th Field Regiment was to be part of the assault course. Training was already under way late in July at Billingshurst, with courses and lectures on water-proofing of vehicles etc.

Training also took place at Inveraray in Scotland and at Poole Harbour and Studland Bay where most of the assault practice landings were made. The new SP (self-propelled) guns and command tanks were beginning to arrive in increasing numbers. This American-made 105mm field gun fired a 35-pound HE shell, mounted on a modified tank chassis of the Sherman type.

Through that winter it was a familiar sight to see the SPs roaring through the streets of Bournemouth, with their seven men crew perched on top beside the gun among the shell cases. These troops were all dressed in black overalls and wore the new assault type steel helmets. The first large waterborne exercise from Bournemouth was Operation *Pirate*. This exercise was considered a pattern upon which all later exercises were fashioned. The run-in was made at Studland Bay, with the guns on the craft opening fire within sight of shore. More exercises off Studland Bay followed, leading up to the more important Exercise *Vidi-Push* on 28 November 1943.

Just before Christmas the regiment moved to Lark Hill, for seven miserably cold days of training. On the return to Bournemouth Lt-Colonel Clifford took command of the Regiment.

In January 1944 another water-borne scheme named Exercise *Cordage* began, in what was known as the final stage of the assault training and where all arms participated. In February the visits started of the distinguished visitors to inspect troops. These dignatories included Major General Keller, followed by General Montgomery, who said to us . . . We are going to see this thing through, you and I. I have never seen so many gunners together at one time before. To see so many is good as it is the gunners that win battles.

In April 1944 the Regiment left Bournemouth and moved to the concentration area at Parkgate in Hampshire, where the final preparations for the invasion were made. Exercise *Trousers* was carried out, which involved an assault landings on Slapton Sands in South Devon. This location was chosen because the area resembled the place where the assault landings were to be made on the Continent. This was followed by Exercise *Fadius*, this was the last full scale exercise before D-Day and just before this exercise His Majesty The King inspected the men.

Two weeks before D-Day a fence was put around the camp area and the Regiment was cu- off from the outside world. On 29 May, at a time when all preparations had been completed, a German plane flew over the area and scored a direct hit with a heavy bomb on one of the SP guns. The explosions and fire set off the contents of the SPs, including mines, small arms, ammunition, grenades, mortar bombs and Piate bombs. The equipment was concentrated in a small space with vehicles parked nose to tail, fully loaded ready to move. The fire soon spread, setting-off the deadly explosives in adjacent vehicles. The men acted quickly, drivers entered the vehicles even though they were burning and drove them to safety through a wall of fire and exploding ammunition. After three hours the fires were brought under control. At times the explosions were so violent that large portions of armoured equipment and a motor-cycle were blown 80-yards. Many houses in the district were wrecked, but no one was killed.

The toll that night was two Sherman tanks, four SPs, a Jeep and three motor-cycles were destroyed. A number of men were Mentioned In Despatches that night. This attack was a great loss to the Regiment, which expected to be fighting within a few days. However within 24 hours new equipment was arriving and the water-proofing and testing began immediately. This task was completed within two days - which had previously taken two weeks. Soon after the loading of vehicles onto landing craft began at Gosport, Stokes Bay and Southampton.

On 1 June 1944 as each landing craft was filled it moved into its allotted place in Southampton Water and finally large camouflage nets were put right over all the crafts. The weather was bad and there we waited, until orders were given to sail on the night of 5 June. The sea was rough, very rough, and every man was sea-sick and I defy any man to say that he was not scared. We did not know what lay ahead, our destiny was *Juno* Beach. We had been told that it was uncleared of mines and to expect 50% casualties. Luckily our casualties were less than that, I was one of the fortunate ones and went through to the end of the war without a scratch.

I would like to add that my son was born on 18 June 1943 and at the time my wife had not heard if I was still alive.

Gunner Frank Lawson K92478, 78 Battery E Troop, 13th Field Regiment, RCA.
Ardingly. April 2002.

BATTLE ABBEY AND CANADIA

A variety of Canadian battalions were stationed around the historic town of Battle in East Sussex in the 1940s and have left an indelible plethora of experiences in the community.

North of the town maps bear the title CANADIA beside the A2100 highway. Research via the local history society and library services has revealed nothing of the origins of the area unfortunately. However history has it prior to the 1914-1918 conflict a Mr A. Rae ran a small mixed farm titled *Le Rette* on Canadian lines for potential emigrants. His pupils studied farming methods and could in time apply for land grants up to 160-acres for farming in the new world.

Post-1919 there were a number of Canadian soldiers who wished to settle in the area and a wooden chalet type community sprang-up off a track east of the A2100 named CANADIA ROAD. Today only a few wooden bungalows remain, as other plots have been eclipsed by modern homes. Close to the start of the road *Canadia House* maintains the link - up to a property named *Quebec* at the end of the road.

PLT.

A soldiers view of the courtyard and archway at Battle Abbey. (Gote House)

READINESS FOR ACTION

Routines and occupation of quarters in Sussex during the spring of 1942 was typified by men of the Princess Louise Dragoon Guards billeted at Bulverhythe, between Hastings and St Leonards from 13 April.

A tactical exercise followed a regimental parade. B squadron of the Princess Louise took actual positions in training, with the officers adding comment the next day. The unit paraded despite heavy rain on the 19th in preparation for a divisional exercise. Major Stroud gave junior officers a lecture late on 18 November, then two days later Sergeant R. Ward presented a demonstration for officers on applications of aircraft models with a lamp and screen to convey aircraft recognition. Major Small, of Home Forces, lectured on combined operations on 8 December. Lieuts Radford and Thorne observed a parade of varied equipment at Crawley in use by the Canadian Army on 15th December. This date was the occasion of the third anniversary of the inaugural landing of Canadian troops in Britain.

The 3rd Field Park Company, Royal Canadian Engineers, demonstrated mine-laying and use of booby-traps at Bexhill Recreation Ground to men on the 21st, 22nd and 23rd December and on the 22nd four officers lectured on infantry fire power. On 5 January Captain H.D.F. Parker spoke to officers on camouflage and concealment. In the evening of 9 March Captain Chambers, from Divisional Intelligence, spoke to officers and NCOs of evasion and escape methods in enemy occupied territory.

On the 16 March Col Adams spoke of his role as an umpire during Operation *Spartan*. On 23 March the Commanding Officer and squadron commanders attended an outdoor demonstration of mine-clearing and the following day 325 all ranks went to an area south of Polegate for demonstrations of German Army tactics and battle drill. A group of men left with their vehicles from Battle railway station for Wemyss Bay, near Glasgow, on 27 November for training in combined operations. On the following day six officers and 201 other ranks left for training at Wemyss Bay, returning on 8 December.

With the exception of the Regimental HQ and Officers Mess the whole unit moved from billets on the outskirts of Hastings and St Leonards on 20 November to nearby postings at Hastings. A Squadron went to the *Adelphi Hotel*, B Squadron to *Regency Mansions* and C went to the *Burlington* with HQ Squadron moving to the *Albion Hotel*. Regimental HQ moved from *Langley Place* to temporary HQ at 26 Holmsdale Road, Hastings, on 26 November.

On 12 December the Light Aid Detachment took over the Fishmarket, and a detail of six NCOs and 50 other ranks moved fishing boats 500-yards away to clear the area. The next day a naval mine was washed ashore 200-yards east from Regimental HQ, but this was soon cleared away.

Eventually a mobilisation order arrived on 27 April when a staff sergeant and 15 other ranks arrived three days later, as a detail, to raise hopes of a move. The unit was officially mobilised by 00.01 hours on 1 May when 288 all ranks under Major Duck left Hastings for Kirkintilloch in Scotland on 5 May. Their 106 vehicles and 91 motor-cycles went via London and Lutterworth to a staging camp at 18.00 hours. Next day the convoy travelled to Preston, then onto Dumfries and Kirkintilloch. Word came through that some kit left with he rear-guard detail was destroyed in the enemy attack on the *Albany Hotel* at Hastings.

The presence of the Princess Louise Dragoon Guards on the south coast was taken over by the 17th Duke of Yorks Hussars, 7th Recce Regiment, who had a tragically torrid time there.

From *The Princess Louise Dragoon Guards* Regimental History.

1940s Shadows on the Ashdown Forest

In my early teens my younger sister Barbara and myself lived at Pump House Farm which comprises of 200-acres a few miles east from East Grinstead. A mile away Canadian troops were later camped around the war-requisitioned Ashplants House that is set on the second highest point in East Sussex and has gorgeous gardens and views down to the coast.

Canadian soldiers Dick and Sam are seen on the haystack, whilst my mother Dorothy Somers drives the tractor. (Mrs Joan Brooker)

The Canadian Provals were stationed there and were really nice people to live alongside. They helped on the farms, as well as digging AA gun sites. After a while these troops were supplemented by our Army and RAF personnel camped on the ridgeways and woodland around Pump House Farm, but the Canadians were the most industrious and overall better behaved. I recall a couple of lads named Sam and Dick who assisted on our farm, they were very fit and healthy, smart and upstanding, and always wore their battledress whilst working.

We had no telephones in those days and relied on word of mouth for news, our farm was a sort of half-way house locally. We had an acid charged wireless for national news and entertainment. Domestic goods were often bartered - rationed marmalade and sugar for butter, milk etc. Sometimes our 10-gallon milk churns were returned with scarce sugar and other rareties inside.

The flying bombs were very frightening. On one occasion a V1 bomb fell in woodland off the Holtye Road and about twenty-five years ago we found relics of the missile still in the corner of the woods. The barrage balloons over Oxted were quite a sight and amazingly they did not entangle, but one day we saw a balloon go up in a puff of smoke.

Our father, Fred Somers, was a great character. Often he appreciated some male company and would take several Canadians over to East Grinstead, in his Austin Seven, to share a couple of pints.

My husband Geoff was 16-17 years old when the war started and joined the RAF in 1942. He recalls lively French Canadian Princess Patricia Light Infantry troops around Brighton, often letting-off steam as any bottled-up soldier needed to at times.

Mrs Joan Brooker, Lancing. May 2002.

Mrs Santa-Cruz indicates the soldiers initials engraved on the beech tree near her home. (Gote House)

CANADIAN TREE ENGRAVINGS

On Hackhurst Farm, close to my home, there is an old beech tree known as *The Canadian Tree* amid bluebell woodland. Personal initials and numbers were carved on the tree trunk by Canadian soldiers stationed in the district in the 1940s, many of these troops were billeted in neighbourhood farms and stately houses. Their vehicles and armoury lay camouflaged under trees around the lanes and fields, whilst they trained or waited overseas postings.

In an almost bizarre scene now, some sixty years later, soldiers' lettering remains on the tree trunk. The lettering looms like ancient hieroglyphics, a legacy distorted by decades of tree growth and weathering, since the troops left the district.

Mrs B. Santa-Cruz, Lower Dicker, Hailsham. May 2002

1940S HORSHAM RE-VISITED

I was stationed in a camp about three miles south of Horsham with the Canadian 3rd Division HQ, during 1942 to early 1944, where I worked as Corporal in the Army Educational Services. On my first visit to Horsham I was attracted to the central band-stand and was befriended by an elderly couple, surname Garman. Later I accompanied them to their hall of service, located at a sharp fork intersection with the main Worthing Road.

There I met a number of people, most of them elderly, whose own sons were serving with the British forces. Mr and Mrs Garman took me home for dinner and a day of relaxation and in spite of rationing the 'vittels' were good. Their own two sons were in the forces, so they became my temporary 'Mum and dad' while there and after. We corresponded for many years after the war, even after 'Dad' died and 'Mum' re-married.

I have re-visited Horsham twice since those army days. The first was in 1972 as an exchange teacher, when I was able to renew some war-time acquaintances with Shipley.

Lewis W. Vath, Surrey, British Columbia. 1994.

(Horsham Museum, Horsham District Council)

Below: Coastal defence in British Columbia. A 9.2-inch gun with 6-pounder sub-calibre mounted for practice at Albert Head Battery, Esquimalt B.C., was erected in 1937. (National Film Board)

Above: Vimy Barracks, Ontario, were built as an unemployment relief project prewar. During the war R.C. Signals and regimental signallers trained at these premises. (Canadian Archives)

FORMING OUR FOLKLORE

Occupation of the nation by Canadian forces has now formed part of our national heritage in various guises.

Ashcombe Toll House, on the A27 at Kingston, near Lewes, dates from the 1820s.

During the early 1940s the property was home for a local personality known unkindly as *Mothball Annie*. The story has it she was run-over and killed one dark night by a Canadian Army lorry during a blackout period. *(PLT)*

EXPERIENCES OF 1940S COUNTRY LIFE

Occupation by Canadian troops of the Possingworth Park acres, near Cross-in-Hand, became part of everyday life in the rural area for children and adults. I worked with the National Fire Service and as such managed to be quite mobile despite rationing and other restrictions. The vast hutted Canadian Army camp at Possingworth had mains drainage and electric lights laid. Tales of soldiers' activities abound still and when they left supposedly an amount of equipment and plant was buried - as happened with other camps, aerodromes etc.

The old Manor House at Possingworth was occupied by Canadian officers. There was no serious damage to the estate, bombs fell and inevitably some troops left their marks about, generally there we no problems. Well-mannered troops would help out in the district, farming, gardening or with social events where they were welcomed. Rare rations, nylon stockings and chocolate etc, were freely passed around at times. Curiously it is said the family of *Lord Haw Haw*, William Joyce, lived close-by at Waldron.

As a member of the NFS we were called to horrific emergencies in London and its suburbs. I might be stationed at Dartford, Burwash, Caterham or Eastbourne during this period that is remembered with some affection for other people and events.

Jack Ashdown, Cross-in-Hand. May 2002

Coastal Towns Attacked

The official overview of *Operation Spartan* of March 1943 was that it was one of the most successful training exercises to date. Troops were up to strength and units had their full quota of armoured cars and Bren gun carriers. Additionally it was the first time a Division had covered such great distance as the assembly progressed from the south coast to the Midlands north of Oxford.

The dramatic realisms of warfare were brought home to some units soon after they settled back in their billets on 29 March. Brighton sustained a heavy raid from light bombers and fighters over the London Road town centre residential area. School children playing in the Preston Park were shot at and troops attending their vehicles, under bordering trees, had little to retaliate with. Railway tracks and parkland was strafed and troops at AA posts had only Bren guns to return enemy fire, until some Spitfires arrived to fend off the enemy.

The Mayor of Brighton formally wrote to Colonel Hugman of the 17th Hussars and his Regiment thanking them for the splendid work they had done saving the children's lives. Another letter went to the Mayor of Montreal to convey Brighton's appreciation to the Montreal citizens whose men had served so effectively in the resort's time of need.

A farewell dance was staged at Brighton's oriental Corn Exchange for the town to say good-bye to the 17th Hussars before they moved to Hastings on 6 May 1943. The pair of seaside resorts are about 15 miles apart and many friendships were continued amicably. Then again possible enemy filtered information led to a coastal town being attacked.

The 17th Hussars, 7th Reconnaissance Regiment, were stationed on Hastings seafront, mainly in requisitioned hotels. There occupation began quite calmly. The Anti-Tank Battery under Captain G.F. Cassidy out-shot the 3rd Anti-Tank Regiment on the ranges on 14 May.

The devastation to Hastings seafront caused by the April 1943 attacks. (Gote House)

Then the 17th Hussars Blue and White hats were taken out and dusted-off for a impressive Wings for Victory parade held in Hastings on 19 May. Then the following Sunday 23 May tragedy struck the south coast again.

About 15 Focke Wolfe 109s came in low from the sea at 12.55 hours, devastating personnel out enjoying the midday sun on the seafront, Old Town and London Road district. The enemy airmen appeared to have advance knowledge of troop locations as bombs exploded central to the Regimental HQ, the YMCA and where the Officers Mess was located in the Queens and Albany hotels. The casualties that day could have been far more serious, but ironically men had requested that their meal be deferred whilst they enjoyed a popular radio broadcast. A Regimental Funeral paraded through the town on 27 May for the 11 men killed in the raid, some 34 troops were wounded in this action. The total dead numbered 25 with civilians and 85 people were injured.

Understandably men of the 17th Hussars were keen to move onto their next posting at West Chiltington, near Pulborough, where they arrived on 5 June. There neat camp at the foot of the Downs was described as ideal. The unit was compact and comprised of Nissen huts and hard-standing. Exercise *Smashex* followed involving Infantry and Armour combined. On 6 August their first heavy armoured cars arrived. These were Canadian-built Foxes with heavy armour plating and Browning .50 and Browning .30 machine guns on their turrets. Up to a week would be consumed on downland firing ranges, before the 17th Hussars moved onto the Nine Yews camp on September 15th that the United States Engineering Corps had left in an immaculate condition.

Adapted from *The 7th Recce Regiment in World War II.*
Via Mrs May Jackson, (ex ATS) Little Common, Bexhill. May 2002.

October 1942 as Canadian divisional troops embark in landing craft at the Cuckmere Haven, Seaford, RCASC Battle School. (National Archives of Canada)

STORRINGTON BESIEGED

The unhurried countryside around Storrington was transformed when Canadian troops moved into the district. Almost overnight they established camps, occupied family mansions and estates, and commandeered training grounds on farms and downland. Local people often felt out-numbered as their peaceful life-style was transformed. A hutted camp was built under the lee of the Downs at Barns Farm, and remnants of this establishment are extant for the casual enquirer.

The Canadians had previously created camps at Heath Common, Fryen Hall, Monkmead Woods, Water Lane, Sandgate and the Parham Park acres were occupied for most of the early 1940s. Vast sand pits of the locale, like those of Hall & Co, provided endless supply for sand-bag demands. The excavated pits then provided ready-made training terrain for the athletic troops, they had been bottled-up for months and the prospect of battle-like activity was generally well-received.

Numerous older West Sussex folk have tales from that period of occupation some sixty years ago - local legends to be shared in many a public house. Remnants of the Canadian Army occupation can still be identified and some rural artefacts may be reflected upon.

Esther Day, Storrington. June 2002.

NOTHING is to be written on this side except the date and signature of the sender. Sentences not required may be erased. If anything else is added the post card will be destroyed.

[Postage must be prepaid on any letter or post card addressed to the sender of this card.]

I am quite well.

~~*I have been admitted into hospital*~~

~~*sick*~~ } *and am going on well.*

~~*wounded*~~ } *and hope to be discharged soon.*

I ~~*am being sent down to the base.*~~

I have received your { *letter dated* July 13th

~~*telegram*~~ „ ....

~~*parcel*~~ „ ....

Letter follows at first opportunity.

~~*I have received no letter from you*~~

~~*lately*~~

~~*for a long*~~ *time.*

Signature only } H.R. Grover

Date ....

Forms/A2042/7.
Wt. 18709/314. 45,000M. 7/41. W. & S. Ld. 51-726. 192326F.

Despite all manner of interferences imaginable HM Field Service, the military postal service, was one of the most efficient functions during the early 1940s.

Opposite: As a form of censorship messages from troops were conveyed simply by striking-out printed lines. (Russell Weller)

Lower: Welcome news from loved ones on war duty were generally received as a good omen. (Russell Weller)

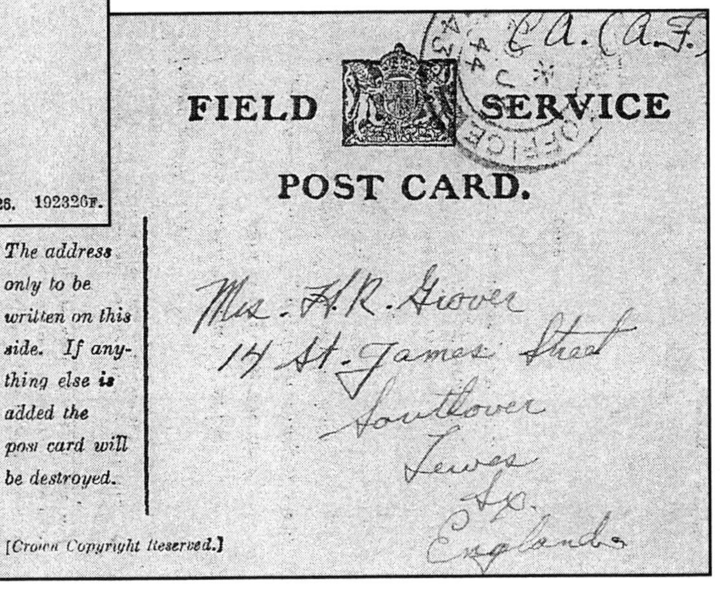

FIELD SERVICE

POST CARD.

The address only to be written on this side. If anything else is added the post card will be destroyed.

Mrs. H.R. Grover
14 St. James Street
Southover
Lewes
Sx.
England

[Crown Copyright Reserved.]

One Friendship, Marriage and War Casualty

Lewes county town was a typical close-knit community into which the Canadian Army descended en masse in the early 1940s. The easy-going attitude of the Canadians soon gelled with the town's people, bringing a rejuvenated vitality of life to the local routines.

My grandfather, Gunner Harold Russell Grover, G4268, 6th Field Regiment RCA, from Fredericton, New Brunswick, was stationed in Manor School in Southover High Street, opposite Anne of Cleves House. Later as Bombardier Grover he moved around the county to Petworth, Worthing and Horsham before going to France and Holland.

Many Lewes properties were taken-over by troops, including the old Manor School where Harold did duty. There he befriended Phyllis Head, (my grandmother) who worked at the Lewes needlemakers factory and who has lived in nearby St James Street all her life.

Harold and Phyllis became Mr and Mrs Grover in Southover Church on 12 February 1944 and my mother Haroldene was born at their St James Street home in November 1945. Harold was often away on exercises with his regiment and then the time came to go overseas. Tragically after going all through those war years, in varying forms of confrontation, Harold, aged 24-years, was killed riding a motor-cycle to an official function in Holland on 19 April 1945. As a war bride grandmother took Haroldene to see Harold's parents, but she returned after a year to Lewes. *Russell Weller, Lewes. June 2002.*

Top: Best man, far right, at their Lewes wedding for Harold and Phyllis Grover was Clarence Whitman, who was also in the Canadian Army. (Russell Weller)

Left: Effervescent Harold shouldered by some regimental comrades during an exercise in Sussex. (Russell Weller)

Right: Harold Grover's first headstone in Holten Cemetery, Holland, where local senior school children adopt a grave to care for. Each Christmas a candle is laid at the Overijssel headstones to create a thought-provoking spectacle. Holten Canadian War Cemetery contains 1,393 Commonwealth burials of the Second World War. (Russell Weller)

LORD STRATHCONA'S HORSE REGIMENT - EXTRACTS

The raid on Dieppe caused a certain amount of stir; because of the fear of reprisal by the Hun. Our tanks were ordered to pull back to the hills north on Hove, to concentrate tactically and be ready for action. On 19 August during a demonstration of a composite regiment, put on for Press correspondents on the Downs, some bombs were dropped a couple of miles away. This excitement undoubtedly detracted from the excellent show under the guiding hand of our CO.

September passed with the same type of training, interrupted only by bad weather. In mid-September we learnt that our popular CO, Lt-Colonel Gianelli, was promoted to the rank of Brigadier and took over command of the 2nd Army Tank Brigade from the 24th September. Our new CO had just recovered from a serious illness, but Lt-Colonel P.G. Griffin soon started to crack the whip in his own imitable fashion. Then on 20 October the unit departed Hove.

More new Ram tanks arrived later that month when we were settled on Maresfield Camp near Uckfield, but the training proved rather poor for tanks and autumn rain added to low in morale. Then towards he close of November somebody in the Desert had made a successful attack in the dark and our routine turned around. Although our stomachs did no agree the night time training proved most successful, even if the locals were not too pleased with the crashes and noise.

In December at Crawley there was commemoration of the third anniversary of the Canadians arriving in Britain, Our part was a memorable parade of painted and polished tanks under Captain Turnley and M. Maisky representing Russia. On 22 December we staged a Christmas Party for the orphans in the Barnado Home at Tunbridge Wells. Christmas Day in the mess officers, led by Brigadier Rutherford, served the seasonal meals.

Then on Boxing Day we were on he move again, back to Hove. Early in the New Year morale was raised when 24 new Ram tanks arrived. The second week saw a divisional reorganisation which eliminated one of the two Armoured Brigades and increased the artillery aspects. The on-going friendly rivalry between the Fort Garrys and 1st Hussars ended when these units left the Division to become part of th new 5th Canadian Armoured Brigade.

John Tillstone, Lewes. June 2002.

SEEN TOWARDS THE SOUTH DOWNS

I live in a house that is part of a rather special Edwardian estate. During the early 1940s our property, with it's octagonal-shaped tower, was commandeered by Canadian troops who used tower as an observation post and billets.

Engraved in the tower are the names and dates of occupying Canadians that add to the intrigue and history of our home, that during those war-torn years had been their home.

Diana Garnier, Broadhill, Kymer. June 2002.

Opposite: Broadhill Tower contains some poignant soldiers engravings. (Gote House)

Top: A curious artefact donated to Horsham Museum, by Redhill CVAUK Branch, is this piece of engraved plywood. The scene is of three French Canadians of the 4th Medical RACASC - drivers from the Canadian clearing Station for Accidents and Wounded medical centre. They were stationed on the corner of Pixcum Lane and the Leatherhead-by-pass in 1942.

The scene features Winston Churchill and American President Franklin D. Roosevelt. (Gote House)

Lower: Canadian troops occupied the Isle of Thorns boys camp at Chelwood Gate on the Ashdown Forest near Crowborough. As a leisure activity soldiers laid decorative tiles around the swimming pool and created an ornate water fountain.

By the turn of the millennium the redundant site was up for sale and the forlorn finale of the soldiers endeavour was recorded at that time.

The construction of a similar swimming pool project, created by Canadian soldiers, at Henfield is being researched. (Gote House)

VIEWED FROM DITCHLING BEACON

Middleton Manor was a Brigade HQ housing many of the ill-fated Dieppe raid troops. Canadians occupied Chichester House amongst others and were generally welcomed in Ditchling, apart from pay night when Military Police were stationed at *The Sandrock*. If invasion seemed imminent, or the Ditchling Beacon terrain especially active, barbed wire was stretched across Beacon Road near Paygate Cottage and residents had to show identity cards. A large gun was fired regularly from Neville Cottages and a large flat field adjoining Molehilly Shaw was protected with tripods and scaffold poles fixed to hawsers. Halfway up the Bostall Canadians had a Nissen hut and dug a trench across the road, filled-in with fougasse bombs, then the highway had to be made safe as invasion threats diminished.

When D-Day orders arrived Canadians poured out of Middleton Manor, leaving huge stocks of hidden explosives to remove. Five Canadians were buried in Plumpton churchyard after crashing a sledge down the scarp near the V woods, five more died unloading ammunition. On a happier note Tommy Langstaff, a warrant officer, married into a local household.

Dick Morley, Ditchling Museum. October 2002.

JOINT HERITAGE PERPETUATED

In common with countless others our home was requisitioned during the early stages of the war for accommodation by Canadians immediately after the Dunkirk evacuations. At the time the house was the stable cottage and mews coach-house for Belmont School, previously known as Clayton Wickham House, that was demolished in 1978.

When we bought our house in 1978 the vendors, who had lived there since 1948, told us of the war-time Canadian presence in the district. They showed us the back of a door, on first floor rear landing, that depicts a maple leaf with the words *Home* apparently drawn by a homesick soldier. We were asked to promise to preserve this and not paint over the mural, which we were of course delighted to do as a form of memorial to the nameless soldier and his comrades.

Other evidence locally of the Canadian Army include rumours of a tank buried in a neighbour's garden, plus at times I unearth .303 bullets whilst gardening.

John Husband, Belmont Lane, Hassocks. July 2002.

Canadian Army artefacts found at John Husband's home. The haunting maple leaf mural, plus varied cartridges - some live - retrieved whilst gardening. (John Husband)

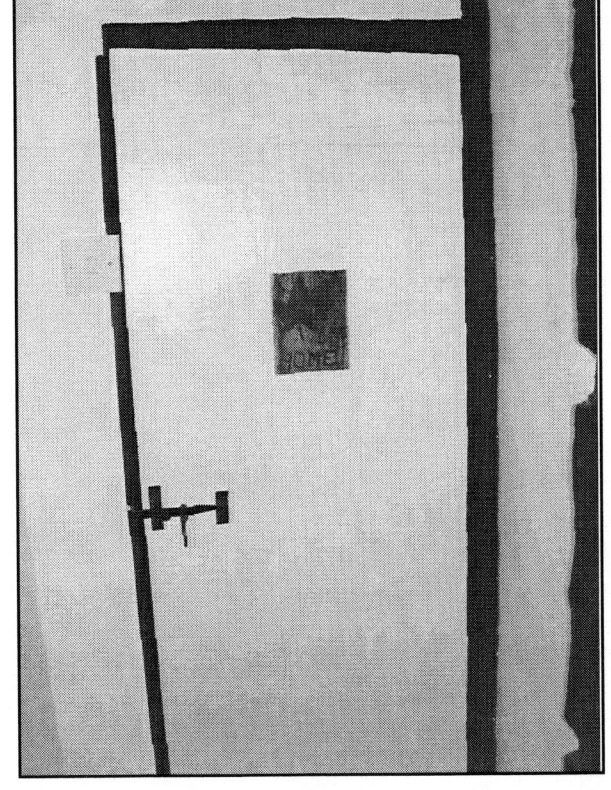

A 1940s Canadian Army mess room in the form of timber hutting, in Underhill Lane past Clayton church, is now a private home. Knowledge of a practice target tank buried near Ditchling Beacon deserves to be investigated further. *(PLT)*

RATIONED FRUITS

In the spring of 1943 my then boyfriend was a corporal in the IV Princess Louise Dragoon Guards, 1st Division, Canadian Army. I was serving in the ATS as a clerk in the RASC Record Office in Hastings and he was stationed in the town. We used to meet by the town centre clock tower as duties permitted.

One summer evening he said had received a parcel from home and in it there was something he wanted to share with me. What could it be I wondered? Firstly we had to walk along to Warrior Square, St Leonards, as he was billeted in the *Adelphi Hotel*. There he left me sitting on a seat, saying he would not be long. He returned with an orange, coated with something looking like candle wax! Great anticipation, would it still be in good condition after its long journey from Saskatchewan? Well glad to say it was perfect, and in fruit starved England, half an orange never tasted so good.

Mrs May Jackson (ex ATS). Little Common, Bexhill. July 2002.

A PASSAGE OF TIME

War emergency roads were created by Army engineers at strategic locations and provided work for troops waiting to go overseas. Seen, in the 1970s is part of the concrete highway laid by Canadian troops linking hospital units at East Surrey Hospital, Redhill, and Clay Lane Nutfield towards Redhill aerodrome. By the time this photo was recorded part of the road, lower left, has visibly been re-claimed for farming and enabled ready-made foundations for barns. *(PLT)*

Apart from numerous colleges and institutional buildings being commandeered as war emergency units many extensions to hospitals were erected, often by Canadian troops. Vast contingency facilities at Chichester, Horsham, East Grinstead and Cuckfield, were amongst the regional units built.

Above and opposite: The Canadian Wing at Queen Victoria Hospital, in East Grinstead, thrives as an important aspect of their now extended facilities. (Gote House)

Lower: The Canadian Wing at the, long redundant, Cuckfield Hospital had been eclipsed by the time of the new millennium. (Gote House)

Roll of Honour

Compiled by Stanley James 1999-2002 from Commonwealth War Graves Commission records, the Canadian Book of Remembrance, Public Record Office files and field trips, together with reference to History of RAF Marine Craft 1918-1986. Canipex. 1987.

The west corner at Brookwood Military Cemetery in Surrey contains approximately 2,400 Canadian graves of the Second World War. Of these plots forty-three are the graves of men who died of injuries during Operation *Jubilee* - The Dieppe Raid.

Maple trees were replaced about six months prior to these scenes being recorded. The original trees had become diseased and bordering pines were overcrowding the cemetery, replacement maples now add a fresh ambience to the setting. The lower scene is of the Canadian Records Building at Brookwood Commonwealth War Graves Commission.

Operation *Jubilee* - The Dieppe Raid

Many authoritative and sensitive accounts of the tragedy that was Dieppe in August 1942 have appeared since the time.

The works of Colonel C.P. Stacey OBE over the years is particularly acknowledged. Latterly in his role as University Professor Emeritus, University of Toronto.

More recently the title DIEPPE, DIEPPE by Brereton Greenhous for Editions Art Global Inc in 1992 is outstanding. The commemorative work was produced in co-operation with National Defence HQ, Ottawa, Canada.

DIEPPE. TRAGEDY TO TRIUMPH
Brigadier General Denis Whitaker DSO and Bar, CM, ED, CD.
McGraw-Hill Ryerson Ltd.
Ontario 1992.

The ill-fated 19 August 1942 dawn frontal attack on the resort of Dieppe raises many contentious issues to this day. The facts are that Canadian soldiers formed the main assault force of the operation, that had been postponed from the July 1942 Operation *Rutter* plans.

Described officially as a reconnaissance force the troops were supposed to capture the lightly-defended port of Dieppe and hold it for 24 hours.

The main embarkation port was Newhaven, plus some Les Fusiliers Mont-Royal from Shoreham.
6,100 all ranks left for the raid. 4,963 were Canadians and about 1,075 were British. Some 50 all ranks from 1st U.S. Ranger Battalion were dispersed as observers. Another 20 men of No 10 (Inter-Allied) Commando made up the force.

The following day 907 Canadians, over 18%, had been slaughtered on the beaches, around the town, or died of their wounds. Some 2.460 men were wounded, 1,874 soldiers were taken prisoner. Only 336 of the 2,210 who returned to England got back unharmed. Between two and three hundred men had not even landed.

The subject of Operation *Jubilee*, the Dieppe Raid, remains an emotive topic of debate to this day.

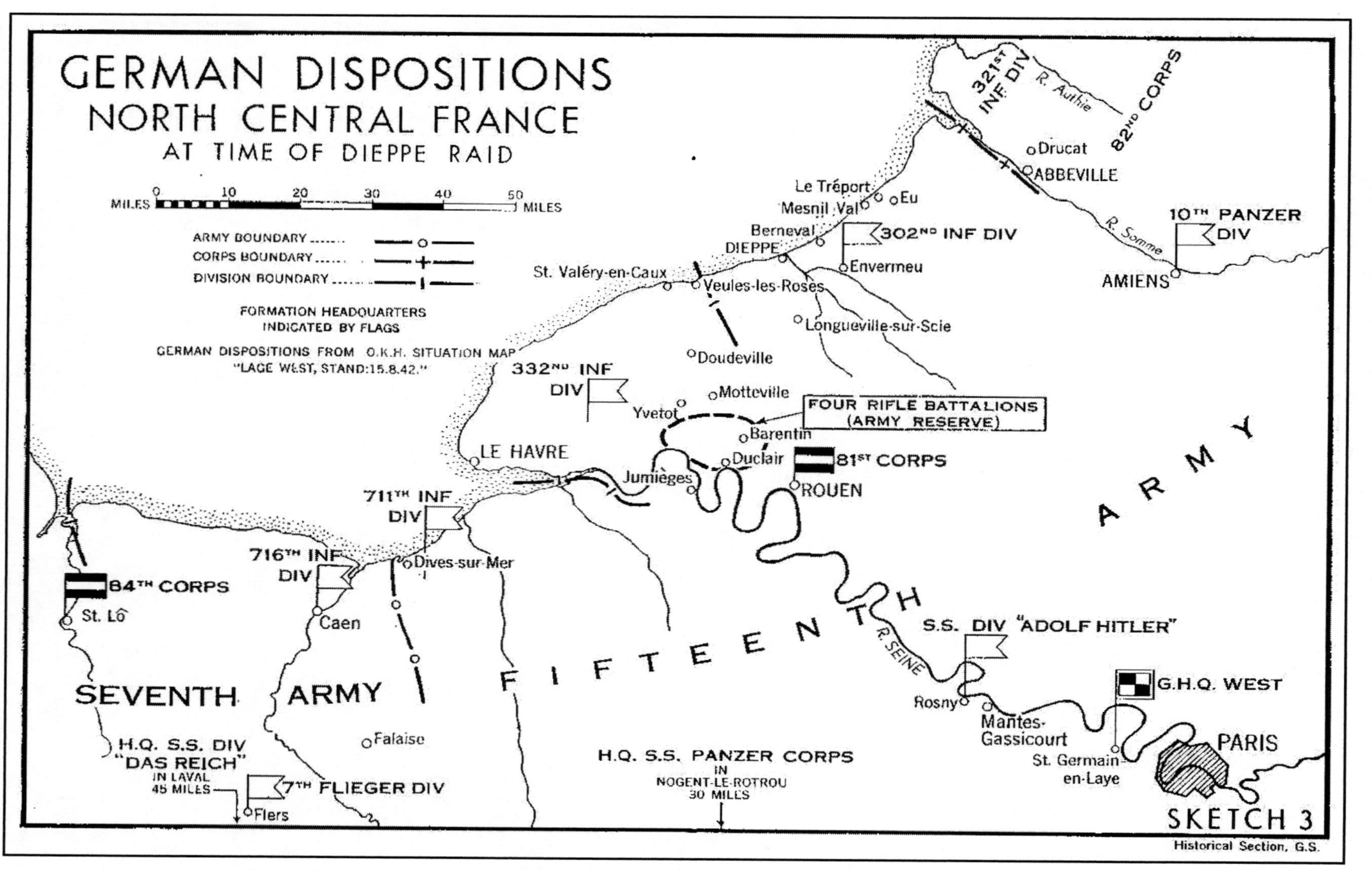

German Dispositions North central France at the time of the Dieppe raid. (Canadian National Archives)

OPERATION *JUBILEE* - ROLL OF HONOUR

Rank.	Name.	Regiment.	Date of Demise.
Pvt.	ABBOTT. J.R.	Royal Hamilton Light Infantry. R.C.I.C.	19th August 1942.
Pvt.	ACTON. E.	Royal Hamilton Light Infantry. R.C.I.C.	19th August 1942.
Pvt.	ADAMS.C.P.	Essex Scottish Regiment. R.C.I.C.	19th August 1942.
Pvt.	ADAMS. E.W.	Royal Regiment of Canada. R.C.I.C.	19th August 1942.
Pvt.	ADAMS. G.C.	Royal Regiment of Canada. R.C.I.C.	19th August 1942.
Pvt.	ADAMS. S.	Royal Regiment of Canada. R.C.I.C.	19th August 1942.
Pvt.	AINSWORTH. E.	Royal Regiment of Canada. R.C.I.C.	19th August 1942.
Pvt.	ALLAN. A.A.	South Saskatchewan Regiment R.C.I.C.	19th August 1942.
Pvt.	ALLEN. E.W.	Essex Scottish Regiment. R.C.I.C.	29th August 1942.
Pvt.	ALLEN. K.W.	Royal Hamilton Light Infantry. R.C.I.C.	19th August 1942.
Tpr.	ALLEN. V.S.	Calgary Regiment. R.C.A.C.	21st August 1942.
Pvt.	ANDREWS. A.	Royal Hamilton Light Infantry. R.C.I.C.	19th August 1942.
Pvt.	ANDERSON. A.	Royal Regiment of Canada. R.C.I.C.	19th August 1942.
Pvt.	ANDERSON. K.W.	Royal Hamilton Light Infantry. R.C.I.C.	19th August 1942.
Pvt.	ANDERSON. L.M.	Royal Hamilton Light infantry. R.C.I.C.	19th August 1942.
Pvt.	ANDREW. L.	Essex Scottish Regiment. R.C.I.C.	19th August 1942.
Lt Col	ANDREWS. J.G.	Calgary Regiment. R.C.A.C.	19th August 1942.
Pvt.	AMBREY.D.G.	Royal Regiment of Canada. R.C.I.C.	19th August 1942.
Pvt.	ARMSTRONG.A.A.	Royal Regiment of Canada. R.C.I.C.	19th August 1942.
Pvt.	ARMSTRONG.T.M.	Royal Regiment of Canada. R.C.I.C.	19th August 1942.
Sgt.	ARTHUR. A.E.	Essex Scottish Regiment. R.C.I.C.	19th August 1942.
Pvt.	ASTLE. T.L.	Royal Regiment of Canada. R.C.I.C.	19th August 1942.
Pvt.	AURAND. J.E.	Essex Scottish Regiment. R.C.I.C.	19th August 1942.
Pvt.	BACHE. W.D.	Royal Regiment of Canada. R.C.I.C.	19th August 1942.
Pvt.	BACHELU. J.H.	South Saskatchewan Regiment R.C.I.C.	19th August 1942.
Pvt.	BAHNUICK.W.	South Saskatchewan Regiment R.C.I.C.	19th August 1942.
Pvt.	BAILEY P.	Royal Regiment of Canada. R.C.I.C.	19th August 1942.
Lt.	BAISLEY. R.S.	Royal Hamilton Light Infantry. R.C.I.C.	19th August 1942.
Pvt.	BAKER. C.A.	Royal Regiment of Canada. R.C.I.C.	19th August 1942.
Pvt.	BALL. M.	Royal Hamilton Light Infantry. R.C.I.C.	19th August 1942.
Pvt.	BALLMER. J.	Essex Scottish Regiment. R.C.I.C.	19th August 1942.
Pvt.	BALOG. J.L.	Essex Scottish Regiment. R.C.I.C.	19th August 1942.
Pvt.	BANKS. D.J.	Royal Regiment of Canada. R.C.I.C.	19th August 1942.
Pvt.	BARBER. A.O.	Royal Hamilton Light Infantry. R.C.I.C.	19th August 1942.
Cpl.	BARBER.W.D.	Royal Hamilton Light Infantry. R.C.I.C.	19th August 1942.
Pvt.	BARNES.F.A.	Royal Hamilton Light Infantry. R.C.I.C.	19th August 1942.
Pvt.	BARNES. H.E.	Royal Canadian Engineers.	19th August 1942.
Pvt.	BARRETT. G.E.	Essex Scottish Regiment. R.C.I.C.	19th August 1942.
Pvt.	BARRETT.H.R.	Toronto Scottish Regiment(M.G)R.C.I.C.	19th August 1942.
Pvt.	BARTON.D.R.	Royal Regiment of Canada. R.C.I.C.	20th August 1942.
Pvt.	BASSETT. G.H.	South Saskatchewan Regiment R.C.I.C.	19th August 1942.
Pvt.	BATEMAN.J.	Royal Regiment of Canada. R.C.I.C.	19th August 1942.
Pvt.	BATHGATE.A.E.	Royal Regiment of Canada. R.C.I.C.	19th August 1942.
Pvt.	BATH. C.F.	Royal Regiment of Canada. R.C.I.C.	19th August 1942.
Pvt.	BAYNE. G.	Q.O.Cameron Highlanders .R.C.I.C.	19th August 1942.
Pvt.	BEATTY.M.D.	South Saskatchewan Regiment R.C.I.C.	19th August 1942.

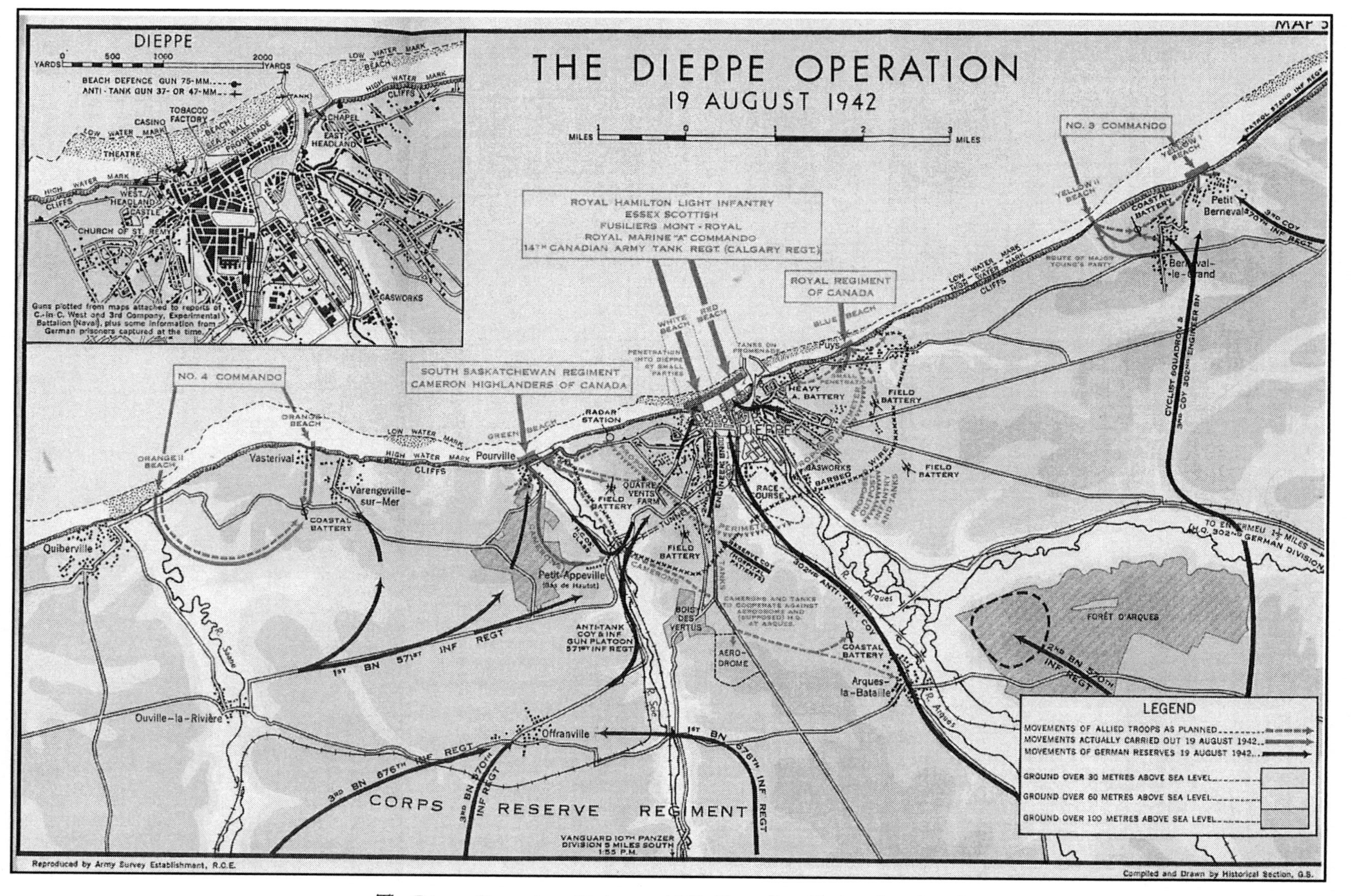

The Dieppe Operation. 19 August 1942. (Canadian National Archives)

OPERATION *JUBILEE* - ROLL OF HONOUR

Pvt.	BEATTY.W.E.	South Saskatchewan Regiment R.C.I.C.	19th August 1942.
"L, Corp"	BEAUDOIN.A.	Les Fusiliers Mont-Royal. R.C.I.C.	19th August 1942.
Sgt.	BEAUDOIN. D.	Les Fusiliers Mont-Royal. R.C.I.C.	19th August 1942.
Pvt.	BELANGER.A.G.	Q.O.Cameron Highlanders R.C.I.C.	19th August 1942.
Pvt.	BELCOURT. R.	Essex Scottish Regiment. R.C.I.C.	19th August 1942.
Pvt.	BELL.H.E.	Royal Hamilton Light Infantry. R.C.I.C.	19th August 1942.
Lt.	BELL.L.C.	Royal Hamilton Light Infantry. R.C.I.C.	19th August 1942.
Pvt.	BELLMORE.O.J.	Royal Regiment of Canada. R.C.I.C.	19th August 1942.
Pvt.	BENDALL.C.H.	Royal Regiment of Canada. R.C.I.C.	19th August 1942.
Pvt.	BENFORD.F.A.	Royal Regiment of Canada. R.C.I.C.	19th August 1942.
Pvt.	BENOIT.D.N.	Q.O.Cameron Highlanders of Canada.R.C.I.C.	19th August 1942.
Pvt.	BERESFORD.E.	Les Fusiliers Mont-Royal. R.C.I.C.	19th August 1942.
Pvt.	BERGER.S.	Essex Scottish Regiment. R.C.I.C.	19th August 1942.
Pvt.	BERTRAND.L.	Les Fusiliers Mont-Royal. R.C.I.C.	19th August 1942.
Pvt.	BEZENAR.G.	Essex Scottish Regiment. R.C.I.C.	19th August 1942.
L.Cpl.	"BINNS.J.E,"	Royal Regiment of Canada. R.C.I.C.	19th August 1942.
Pvt.	BISSON.J.A.	Les Fusiliers Mont-Royal. R.C.I.C.	19th August 1942.
Pvt.	BIZOVY.F.	Essex Scottish Regiment. R.C.I.C.	19th August 1942.
Pvt.	BLACK.W.W.	Essex Scottish Regiment. R.C.I.C.	19th August 1942.
Pvt.	BLEEMAN.M.I.	Royal Hamilton Light Infantry. R.C.I.C.	19th August 1942.
Pvt.	BLOOMFIELD.G.P.	Royal Regiment of Canada. R.C.I.C.	19th August 1942.
Pvt.	BOAL. H.	Q.O.Cameron Highlanders of Canada.R.C.I.C.	19th August 1942.
Pvt.	BOHNERT.L.	Royal Hamilton Light Infantry. R.C.I.C.	19th August 1942.
Pvt.	BOILEAU.M.	Les Fusiliers Mont-Royal. R.C.I.C.	21st August 1942.
Pvt.	BOILY.L.	Les Fusiliers Mont-Royal. R.C.I.C.	19th August 1942.
Sgt.	BOIVIN.A.	Les Fusiliers Mont-Royal. R.C.I.C.	19th August 1942.
Pvt.	BOLITHO.J.E.	Royal Regiment of Canada. R.C.I.C.	19th August 1942.
Pvt.	BOOK. C.	Royal Hamilton Light Infantry. R.C.I.C.	19th August 1942.
Pvt.	BORYS.S	South Saskatchewan Regiment R.C.I.C.	19th August 1942.
Pvt.	BOULANGER.F.	Les Fusiliers Mont-Royal. R.C.I.C.	19th August 1942.
Pvt.	BOULANGER.R.	Les Fusiliers Mont-Royal. R.C.I.C.	19th August 1942.
Pvt.	BOWERS.C.O.	Essex Scottish Regiment. R.C.I.C.	19th August 1942.
Pvt.	BOWMAN.A.E.	Royal Hamilton Light Infantry. R.C.I.C.	19th August 1942.
Pvt.	BOYDEN.H.G.	Essex Scottish Regiment. R.C.I.C.	19th August 1942.
Pvt.	BRADFORD.E.W.	Royal Regiment of Canada. R.C.I.C.	19th August 1942.
Pvt.	BRANT.E.J.	Royal Hamilton Light Infantry. R.C.I.C.	19th August 1942.
Pvt.	BRENNAN.K.P.	Royal Hamilton Light Infantry. R.C.I.C.	19th August 1942.
L.Cpl.	BRENNAND.G.F.	South Saskatchewan Regiment R.C.I.C.	1st August 1942.
Pvt.	BRIGGS.D.S.	Royal Regiment of Canada. R.C.I.C.	19th August 1942.
Pvt.	BRITT.J.C.	Royal Regiment of Canada. R.C.I.C.	19th August 1942.
Pvt.	BROOKS.R.	Royal Regiment of Canada. R.C.I.C.	19th August 1942.
Cpl.	BROWN.A.	Royal Regiment of Canada. R.C.I.C.	19th August 1942.
Pvt.	BROWN.F.O.	Royal Regiment of Canada. R.C.I.C.	19th August 1942.
Pvt.	BROWN.R.R.	Royal Regiment of Canada. R.C.I.C.	19th August 1942.
Pvt.	BROWN.S.	Royal Regiment of Canada. R.C.I.C.	19th August 1942.
Sgl.	BROWNE.W.J.	Royal Canadian Corps of Signals.	19th August 1942.
Pvt.	BRUCE.R.	Royal Hamilton Light Infantry. R.C.I.C.	28th August 1942.
Sgt.	BRUNET.A.	Les Fusiliers Mont-Royal. R.C.I.C.	19th August 1942.
Pvt.	BRUNET.L.	Les Fusiliers Mont-Royal. R.C.I.C.	19th August 1942.

OPERATION *JUBILEE* - ROLL OF HONOUR

Pvt.	BRYAN.R.D.	Royal Regiment of Canada. R.C.I.C.	19th August 1942.
L.Cpl.	BUBIS.M.	Royal Regiment of Canada. R.C.I.C.	19th August 1942.
Pvt.	BUCHANAN.N.L.	Royal Regiment of Canada. R.C.I.C.	19th August 1942.
Pvt.	BURCOMBE. A.G.	Royal Canadian Army Medical Corps.	19th August 1942.
Pvt.	BURKE.C.	Les Fusiliers Mont-Royal. R.C.I.C.	19th August 1942.
Pvt.	BURNETT.J.	Royal Regiment of Canada. R.C.I.C.	19th August 1942.
Pvt.	BURNS.R.G.	South Saskatchewan Regiment R.C.I.C.	19th August 1942.
Pvt.	BUTLER.L.J.	Royal Hamilton Light Infantry. R.C.I.C.	19th August 1942.
Pvt.	BUTLER.R.C.	Royal Hamilton Light Infantry. R.C.I.C.	19th August 1942.
Pvt.	BYKLUM.A.	South Saskatchewan Regiment R.C.I.C.	19th August 1942.
Pvt.	CAISSE.G.	Les Fusiliers Mont-Royal. R.C.I.C.	19th August 1942.
Pvt.	CALBERG.H.R.	Essex Scottish Regiment. R.C.I.C.	19th August 1942.
Pvt.	CALWAY.E.G.	Royal Regiment of Canada. R.C.I.C.	19th August 1942.
Pvt.	CAMERON.W.L.	South Saskatchewan Regiment R.C.I.C.	19th August 1942.
Pvt.	CAMPBELL.J.D.	South Saskatchewan Regiment R.C.I.C.	19th August 1942.
L Cpl.	CAMPBELL.S.	South Saskatchewan Regiment R.C.I.C.	19th August 1942.
Pvt.	CARDINAL.A	Les Fusiliers Mont-Royal. R.C.I.C.	19th August 1942.
Pvt.	CARDINAL.R.	Les Fusiliers Mont-Royal. R.C.I.C.	19th August 1942.
Lt.	CARPENTER.F.B.	Royal Canadian Artillery.	19th August 1942.
Sgl.	CARRIER.W	Royal Canadian Corps of Signals.	19th August 1942.
Pvt.	CARRIERE.J.L.	Les Fusiliers Mont-Royal. R.C.I.C.	19th August 1942.
Cpl.	CARROLL.M.T.	Royal Regiment of Canada. R.C.I.C.	19th August 1942.
Pvt.	CARSWELL.R.	Q.O.Cameron Highlanders of Canada.R.C.I.C.	19th August 1942.
Pvt.	CARSWELL.R.	South Saskatchewan Regiment R.C.I.C.	19th August 1942.
Pvt.	CARTER.L.E.	Royal Hamilton Light Infantry. R.C.I.C.	19th August 1942.
Pvt.	CARVER.H.A.	Q.O.Cameron Highlanders of Canada.R.C.I.C.	19th August 1942.
Pvt.	CAYEN.A.	South Saskatchewan Regiment R.C.I.C.	19th August 1942.
Pvt.	CHADWICK.S.	Royal Hamilton Light Infantry. R.C.I.C.	19th August 1942.
Pvt.	CHAMPAGNE.R.	Les Fusiliers Mont-Royal. R.C.I.C.	19th August 1942.
Bom.	CHARTERS.J.	Royal Canadian Artillery.	19th August 1942.
Pvt.	CHEVALIER.A.	Les Fusiliers Mont-Royal. R.C.I.C.	19th August 1942.
Pvt.	CHILCOTT.W.J.	Royal Hamilton Light Infantry. R.C.I.C.	19th August 1942.
Pvt.	CHILTON.L.R.	South Saskatchewan Regiment R.C.I.C.	19th August 1942.
L Cpl.	CHOQUETTE.G.	Les Fusiliers Mont-Royal. R.C.I.C.	19th August 1942.
Pvt.	CHYMKO.W.D.	South Saskatchewan Regiment R.C.I.C.	19th August 1942.
Sgt.	CLARK.C.B.	South Saskatchewan Regiment R.C.I.C.	19th August 1942.
Cpl.	CLARKE.I.	Essex Scottish Regiment. R.C.I.C.	19th August 1942.
Pvt.	CLARKE.I.	Royal Hamilton Light Infantry. R.C.I.C.	19th August 1942.
Pvt.	CLARKE.J.A.	South Saskatchewan Regiment R.C.I.C.	19th August 1942.
Pvt.	CLAUSEN.R.L.	Royal Hamilton Light Infantry. R.C.I.C.	26th August 1942.
Pvt.	CLEMMENS.H.R.	Royal Regiment of Canada. R.C.I.C.	19th August 1942.
Pvt.	CLOUTIER.M.	Essex Scottish Regiment. R.C.I.C.	19th August 1942.
Cpl.	CLOWES.F	South Saskatchewan Regiment R.C.I.C.	19th August 1942.
Pvt.	"COAT.T,C."	Royal Hamilton Light Infantry. R.C.I.C.	19th August 1942.
Pvt.	COFFEY.J.	Royal Regiment of Canada. R.C.I.C.	19th August 1942.
Pvt.	COHEN.L.	Royal Regiment of Canada. R.C.I.C.	19th August 1942.
L.Cpl.	COLE.A.G.	Royal Hamilton Light Infantry. R.C.I.C.	19th August 1942.
Pvt.	COLEMAN.E.B.	Royal Hamilton Light Infantry. R.C.I.C.	19th August 1942.
Pvt.	COLEMAN.H.A.	Royal Hamilton Light Infantry. R.C.I.C.	19th August 1942.

OPERATION *JUBILEE* - ROLL OF HONOUR

Pvt.	COLLINS.R.	South Saskatchewan Regiment R.C.I.C.	19th August 1942.
Pvt.	COLLISON.C.K.	Essex Scottish Regiment. R.C.I.C.	19th August 1942.
Cpl.	COLTMAN.J.	Royal Hamilton Light Infantry. R.C.I.C.	19th August 1942.
Pvt.	CONICK.P.	Royal Hamilton Light Infantry. R.C.I.C.	19th August 1942.
W.O.II.	CONNOLLY.B.	Q.O.Cameron Highlanders of Canada.R.C.I.C.	19th August 1942.
Pvt.	COOK.N.W.	Essex Scottish Regiment. R.C.I.C.	19th August 1942.
Pvt.	COPEMAN.J.L.	Royal Hamilton Light Infantry. R.C.I.C.	19th August 1942.
Pvt.	CORMIER.A.R.	Essex Scottish Regiment. R.C.I.C.	19th August 1942.
Pvt.	COTTINGTON.G.S.	Royal Hamilton Light Infantry. R.C.I.C.	19th August 1942.
L.Cpl.	COULTER.J.S.	Q.O.Cameron Highlanders of Canada.R.C.I.C.	19th August 1942.
Pvt.	COUVIA.E.	Essex Scottish Regiment. R.C.I.C.	19th August 1942.
Sap.	COWLISHAW.F.	Royal Canadian Engineers	19th August 1942.
L.Sgt.	CRABTREE.C.	Royal Regiment of Canada. R.C.I.C.	19th August 1942.
Pvt.	CRONIN.J.B.	Royal Hamilton Light Infantry. R.C.I.C.	19th August 1942.
Pvt.	CRONIN.L.G.	Royal Regiment of Canada. R.C.I.C.	19th August 1942.
Pvt.	CRONIN.M.T.	Royal Hamilton Light Infantry. R.C.I.C.	19th August 1942.
Pvt.	CROSSLEY.W.E.	Royal Regiment of Canada. R.C.I.C.	19th August 1942.
Sgt.	CRUICKSHANK.G.M.	Royal Hamilton Light Infantry. R.C.I.C.	19th August 1942.
Pvt.	CUDMORE.A.M.	Essex Scottish Regiment. R.C.I.C.	19th August 1942.
Pvt.	CUNNINGHAM.A.E.	Royal Regiment of Canada. R.C.I.C.	19th August 1942.
Pvt.	DALLAIRE.M.	Les Fusiliers Mont-Royal. R.C.I.C.	19th August 1942.
Pvt.	DANCHUK.W.	South Saskatchewan Regiment R.C.I.C.	19th August 1942.
Pvt.	DANFORTH.G.A.	South Saskatchewan Regiment R.C.I.C.	19th August 1942.
Pvt.	DAVIDSON.R.D.	Essex Scottish Regiment. R.C.I.C.	19th August 1942.
Pvt.	DAVIES.L.O.	South Saskatchewan Regiment R.C.I.C.	19th August 1942.
Pvt.	DAVIS.G.H.	Royal Regiment of Canada. R.C.I.C.	19th August 1942.
Pvt.	DAVIS.H.W.T.	Royal Regiment of Canada. R.C.I.C.	19th August 1942.
Pvt.	DAVISON.W.W.	South Saskatchewan Regiment R.C.I.C.	19th August 1942.
Lt.	DAWSON.A.F.	South Saskatchewan Regiment R.C.I.C.	19th August 1942.
Pvt.	DAWSON.F.A.	Essex Scottish Regiment. R.C.I.C.	19th August 1942.
Pvt.	DAY.C.H.	Royal Hamilton Light Infantry. R.C.I.C.	19th August 1942.
Sgl.	DEAN.T.M.	Royal Canadian Corps of Signals.	19th August 1942.
Pvt.	DEMPSEY.D.T.	South Saskatchewan Regiment R.C.I.C.	19th August 1942.
Pvt.	DEPELTEAU.C.E.	Les Fusiliers Mont-Royal. R.C.I.C.	19th August 1942.
Pvt.	DESORMIERS.A.	Les Fusiliers Mont-Royal. R.C.I.C.	19th August 1942.
Cpl.	DESROCHES.J.	Les Fusiliers Mont-Royal. R.C.I.C.	19th August 1942.
Pvt.	DICKENSON.H.D.	Royal Regiment of Canada. R.C.I.C.	21st August 1942.
Pvt.	DICUS.H.E.	Royal Hamilton Light Infantry. R.C.I.C.	19th August 1942.
Capt.	DILLON.G.W.R.	Les Fusiliers Mont-Royal. R.C.I.C.	19th August 1942.
Pvt.	DION.L..	Les Fusiliers Mont-Royal. R.C.I.C.	19th August 1942.
Pvt.	DIXON.G.A.	Essex Scottish Regiment. R.C.I.C.	19th August 1942.
C/Q.Sgt.	DONALD.C.	Essex Scottish Regiment. R.C.I.C.	19th August 1942.
Cpl.	DONNELLY.E.R.	Essex Scottish Regiment. R.C.I.C.	19th August 1942.
Pvt.	DOONAN.B.D.	Royal Regiment of Canada. R.C.I.C.	19th August 1942.
Pvt.	DORVAL.N.	Royal Regiment of Canada. R.C.I.C.	19th August 1942.
Pvt.	DOUGLAS.H	Q.O.Cameron Highlanders of Canada.R.C.I.C.	19th August 1942.
Pvt.	DUBE.L	Les Fusiliers Mont-Royal. R.C.I.C.	19th August 1942.
Pvt.	DUBOIS.H	Les Fusiliers Mont-Royal. R.C.I.C.	19th August 1942.

OPERATION *JUBILEE* - ROLL OF HONOUR

Pvt.	DUBUC.R	Les Fusiliers Mont-Royal. R.C.I.C.	19th August 1942.
Sgt.	DUCKWORTH.A.H	Royal Regiment of Canada. R.C.I.C.	19th August 1942.
Pvt.	DUFOUR.H.	Les Fusiliers Mont-Royal. R.C.I.C.	19th August 1942.
Cpl.	DUFRESNE.J.R	Les Fusiliers Mont-Royal. R.C.I.C.	19th August 1942.
Pvt.	DUGGAN.J.A	Q.O.Cameron Highlanders of Canada.R.C.I.C.	19th August 1942.
Pvt.	DUNCAN.A	Essex Scottish Regiment. R.C.I.C.	19th August 1942.
Pvt.	DUNKIN.W	Q.O.Cameron Highlanders of Canada.R.C.I.C.	19th August 1942.
L Cpl.	DUPUIS.A	Les Fusiliers Mont-Royal. R.C.I.C.	19th August 1942.
Pvt.	DUROCHER.C	Essex Scottish Regiment. R.C.I.C.	19th August 1942.
Pvt.	EAST.C.P	Essex Scottish Regiment. R.C.I.C.	20th August 1942.
Capt.	EATON.E.R.	Les Fusiliers Mont-Royal. R.C.I.C.	19th August 1942.
Pvt.	EDWARDS.W.	Royal Regiment of Canada. R.C.I.C.	19th August 1942.
Capt.	ELLIOT.C.T	Essex Scottish Regiment. R.C.I.C.	2nd September 1942
Sap.	ELLIOT.D.A	Royal Canadian Engineers.	19th August 1942.
Sgt.	EMARTON.G.	Royal Regiment of Canada. R.C.I.C.	19th August 1942.
Cpl.	EMBERSON.C.	Royal Hamilton Light Infantry. R.C.I.C.	19th August 1942.
Pvt.	EMPERINGHAM.A.J.	South Saskatchewan Regiment R.C.I.C.	19th August 1942.
Pvt.	EVANS.L.	Royal Regiment of Canada. R.C.I.C.	19th August 1942.
Pvt.	EVERNDEN.L.	South Saskatchewan Regiment R.C.I.C.	19th August 1942.
Pvt.	FAILLE.A.J.A.	Les Fusiliers Mont-Royal. R.C.I.C.	19th August 1942.
Lt.	FAIRWEATHER.M.E.	Royal Canadian Artillery.	19th August 1942.
Pvt.	FAUBERT.G.R.	Essex Scottish Regiment. R.C.I.C.	19th August 1942.
Pvt.	FERGUSON.R.G.	Q.O.Cameron Highlanders of Canada.R.C.I.C.	19th August 1942.
Pvt.	FERRON.F.	Les Fusiliers Mont-Royal. R.C.I.C.	19th August 1942.
Pvt.	FIEST.M.H.	Royal Regiment of Canada. R.C.I.C.	19th August 1942.
Pvt.	FILION.A.	Les Fusiliers Mont-Royal. R.C.I.C.	19th August 1942.
Pvt.	FILION.R.	Les Fusiliers Mont-Royal. R.C.I.C.	19th August 1942.
Pvt.	FINLEY.J.L.	Royal Regiment of Canada. R.C.I.C.	19th August 1942.
Pvt.	FLANAGAN.J.P.	Royal Hamilton Light Infantry. R.C.I.C.	19th August 1942.
Pvt.	GUBBINS.R.W	Royal Hamilton Light Infantry. R.C.I.C.	19th August 1942.
Pvt.	GUERIN.G	Les Fusiliers Mont-Royal. R.C.I.C.	19th August 1942.
Pvt.	GULLIVER.L.W	Essex Scottish Regiment. R.C.I.C.	19th August 1942.
Pvt.	GURDEN.G.W	Royal Hamilton Light Infantry. R.C.I.C.	19th August 1942.
Pvt.	HADFIELD.V.G	Q.O.Cameron Highlanders of Canada.R.C.I.C.	19th August 1942.
Pvt.	HAGGERTY.C	Royal Regiment of Canada. R.C.I.C.	19th August 1942.
Pvt.	HAINES.R.T.	Essex Scottish Regiment. R.C.I.C.	19th August 1942.
L Cpl.	HAMEL.L	Les Fusiliers Mont-Royal. R.C.I.C.	19th August 1942.
Gnr.	HAMM.A.H.	Royal Canadian Artillery.	19th August 1942.
Pvt.	HANKINSON.L	Royal Hamilton Light Infantry. R.C.I.C.	19th August 1942.
Pvt.	HANSON.P.C.	Essex Scottish Regiment. R.C.I.C.	19th August 1942.
Pvt.	HARMAN.E.A.	South Saskatchewan Regiment R.C.I.C.	19th August 1942.
Pvt.	HARMAN.G.H.	Essex Scottish Regiment. R.C.I.C.	19th August 1942.
Pvt.	HARNEY.F.E.	Royal Regiment of Canada. R.C.I.C.	19th August 1942.
W.O.II.	HARRIS.L.A	Royal Hamilton Light Infantry. R.C.I.C.	19th August 1942.
L Cpl.	HARRIS.S.H.	Royal Hamilton Light Infantry. R.C.I.C.	19th August 1942.
Sgt.	HARRISSON.C	Les Fusiliers Mont-Royal. R.C.I.C.	19th August 1942.
Gnr.	HARTLIN.I.	Royal Canadian Artillery.	19th August 1942.
Cpl.	HATCH.E.T.P.	Q.O.Cameron Highlanders of Canada.R.C.I.C.	19th August 1942.
Pvt.	HAWES.W.	Royal Regiment of Canada. R.C.I.C.	19th August 1942.

OPERATION *JUBILEE* - ROLL OF HONOUR

Maj.	HAYHURST.T.E.	Essex Scottish Regiment. R.C.I.C.	19th August 1942.
Pvt.	HEATHMAN.L	Q.O.Cameron Highlanders of Canada.R.C.I.C.	19th August 1942.
Pvt.	HEBERT.V.	Essex Scottish Regiment. R.C.I.C.	19th August 1942.
Pvt.	HEIFETZ.L.	Royal Hamilton Light Infantry. R.C.I.C.	19th August 1942.
Pvt.	HEINZ.J.	South Saskatchewan Regiment R.C.I.C.	19th August 1942.
L Cpl.	HEINZMAN.W.C.	South Saskatchewan Regiment R.C.I.C.	19th August 1942.
Pvt.	HENDERSON.J.	Royal Hamilton Light Infantry. R.C.I.C.	19th August 1942.
Cpl.	HENDERSON.M.H.	Royal Hamilton Light Infantry. R.C.I.C.	19th August 1942.
Pvt.	HENDRY.A.R.	Royal Regiment of Canada. R.C.I.C.	19th August 1942.
Pvt.	HENRY.N.W.	Royal Hamilton Light Infantry. R.C.I.C.	19th August 1942.
Cpl.	HICKS.F.R.G.	Q.O.Cameron Highlanders of Canada.R.C.I.C.	19th August 1942.
Pvt.	HIGGINS.D.B.	Royal Regiment of Canada. R.C.I.C.	28th August 1942.
Sgt.	HILLIER.E.H.	Royal Regiment of Canada. R.C.I.C.	19th August 1942.
L Cpl.	HIND. A.	Essex Scottish Regiment. R.C.I.C.	19th August 1942.
Pvt.	HILL.C.	Royal Regiment of Canada. R.C.I.C.	19th August 1942.
Sgl.	HILT.G.E.	Royal Canadian Corps of Signals.	19th August 1942.
Pvt.	HOCH.G.F.	Essex Scottish Regiment. R.C.I.C.	19th August 1942.
Cpl.	HODSON.A.E.	Royal Hamilton Light Infantry. R.C.I.C.	19th August 1942.
W.O.II.	HOGUE.L.G.	Les Fusiliers Mont-Royal. R.C.I.C.	19th August 1942.
Pvt.	HOLMES.J.B.	Royal Hamilton Light Infantry. R.C.I.C.	19th August 1942.
W.O.II.	HOLOHAN.J.A.	Royal Regiment of Canada. R.C.I.C.	19th August 1942.
Pvt.	HOOD.S	Royal Regiment of Canada. R.C.I.C.	19th August 1942.
Pvt.	HOOD.T.E.	Essex Scottish Regiment. R.C.I.C.	19th August 1942.
Pvt.	HOUSER.S.K.	Royal Regiment of Canada. R.C.I.C.	19th August 1942.
L.Cpl.	HOWARTH.L.	Royal Hamilton Light Infantry. R.C.I.C.	19th August 1942.
Cpl.	HOWICK.D.L.	Royal Regiment of Canada. R.C.I.C.	19th August 1942.
Cpl.	HUFFMAN.H	Royal Regiment of Canada. R.C.I.C.	19th August 1942.
Pvt.	HUGHAN.J.	Royal Regiment of Canada. R.C.I.C.	19th August 1942.
Pvt.	HUGHES.P.	Royal Hamilton Light Infantry. R.C.I.C.	19th August 1942.
Pvt.	HUNTER.J.J.	Q.O.Cameron Highlanders of Canada.R.C.I.C.	19th August 1942.
Sgt.	HURST.L.E.	Q.O.Cameron Highlanders of Canada.R.C.I.C.	19th August 1942.
Pvt.	HUTSON.A.	Royal Regiment of Canada. R.C.I.C.	3rd September 1942.
Pvt.	HYSERT.F.O.	Royal Hamilton Light Infantry. R.C.I.C.	19th August 1942.
Pvt.	INGRAM.K.J.	Royal Regiment of Canada. R.C.I.C.	19th August 1942.
Pvt.	IRVEN.W.J.	Royal Hamilton Light Infantry. R.C.I.C.	19th August 1942.
W.O.II.	JACOBS.W.S.M.	Royal Regiment of Canada. R.C.I.C.	19th August 1942.
Pvt.	JASIN.W.	South Saskatchewan Regiment R.C.I.C.	19th August 1942.
Pvt.	JELSO.G.J.	Essex Scottish Regiment. R.C.I.C.	19th August 1942.
Pvt.	JEPSEN.H.E.	Essex Scottish Regiment. R.C.I.C.	19th August 1942.
Pvt.	JEWELL.F.	South Saskatchewan Regiment R.C.I.C.	19th August 1942.
Pvt.	JODDIN.D.	Les Fusiliers Mont-Royal. R.C.I.C.	19th August 1942.
Pvt.	JOHNSON.A.E.	Royal Hamilton Light Infantry. R.C.I.C.	19th August 1942.
Pvt.	JOHNSON.R.E.	Royal Regiment of Canada. R.C.I.C.	19th August 1942.
Pvt.	JOHNSTONE.J.E.	South Saskatchewan Regiment R.C.I.C.	19th August 1942.
Pvt.	JONES.C.S.	Royal Hamilton Light Infantry. R.C.I.C.	19th August 1942.
Sgt.	JONES.N.	Royal Regiment of Canada. R.C.I.C.	19th August 1942.
Pvt.	JONES.O.E.	Royal Regiment of Canada. R.C.I.C.	19th August 1942.
Pvt.	JORDAN.W.H.	Royal Regiment of Canada. R.C.I.C.	19th August 1942.
Pvt.	JUDD.H.R.	Royal Hamilton Light Infantry. R.C.I.C.	19th August 1942.

OPERATION *JUBILEE* - ROLL OF HONOUR

Cpl.	JUHLKE.W.H.	Royal Hamilton Light Infantry. R.C.I.C.	19th August 1942.
Pvt.	KAMMERER.G.F.M.	South Saskatchewan Regiment R.C.I.C.	19th August 1942.
Pvt.	KEESLER.C.T.	Royal Regiment of Canada. R.C.I.C.	19th August 1942.
Pvt.	KEELAR.C.H.	Royal Hamilton Light Infantry. R.C.I.C.	19th August 1942.
Pvt.	"KELLY.P.J."	Royal Regiment of Canada. R.C.I.C.	19th August 1942.
Lt.	KEMPTON.L.G.	South Saskatchewan Regiment R.C.I.C.	19th August 1942.
Pvt.	KENNEDY.G.H.	Essex Scottish Regiment. R.C.I.C.	19th August 1942.
L.Cpl.	KENNEDY.W.	Royal Hamilton Light Infantry. R.C.I.C.	19th August 1942.
Pvt.	KENNEDY.W.D.	Essex Scottish Regiment. R.C.I.C.	19th August 1942.
Pvt.	KERR.R.I.	South Saskatchewan Regiment R.C.I.C.	19th August 1942.
Pvt.	KERSLAKE.G.	Royal Hamilton Light Infantry. R.C.I.C.	19th August 1942.
Pvt.	KING.L.J.	South Saskatchewan Regiment R.C.I.C.	19th August 1942.
Pvt.	KING.M.J.	Royal Hamilton Light Infantry. R.C.I.C.	19th August 1942.
Sgt.	KING.R.A.	Q.O.Cameron Highlanders of Canada.R.C.I.C.	26th August 1942.
Pvt.	KIRK.D.J.G.	Q.O.Cameron Highlanders of Canada.R.C.I.C.	19th August 1942.
L.Cpl.	KLASSEN.G.F.	Royal Regiment of Canada. R.C.I.C.	19th August 1942.
Pvt.	KNAPP.H.	Essex Scottish Regiment. R.C.I.C.	19th August 1942.
L.Cpl.	KNIGHT.W.J.	South Saskatchewan Regiment R.C.I.C.	19th August 1942.
Pvt.	KOTTERMAN.G.	Royal Hamilton Light Infantry. R.C.I.C.	19th August 1942.
Pvt.	LABELLE.J.	Les Fusiliers Mont-Royal. R.C.I.C.	19th August 1942.
Pvt.	LACELLE.H.	Les Fusiliers Mont-Royal. R.C.I.C.	19th August 1942.
Pvt.	LAING.A.J.	Q.O.Cameron Highlanders of Canada.R.C.I.C.	19th August 1942.
Pvt.	LAKE.W.J.	Royal Hamilton Light Infantry. R.C.I.C.	19th August 1942.
Pvt.	LALANNE.A.	Les Fusiliers Mont-Royal. R.C.I.C.	19th August 1942.
L.Bom.	LALONDE.F.H.	Royal Canadian Artillery.	19th August 1942.
Pvt.	LAMB.J.O.	Royal Regiment of Canada. R.C.I.C.	19th August 1942.
Pvt.	LANDRIAULT.E	Les Fusiliers Mont-Royal. R.C.I.C.	19th August 1942.
Pvt.	LANDRY.L.	Les Fusiliers Mont-Royal. R.C.I.C.	19th August 1942.
Cpl.	LANGEVIN.M.	Les Fusiliers Mont-Royal. R.C.I.C.	19th August 1942.
Sgt.	LAPOINTE.J.M.A.	Les Fusiliers Mont-Royal. R.C.I.C.	19th August 1942.
L.Sgt.	LAPOINTE.M.	Les Fusiliers Mont-Royal. R.C.I.C.	19th August 1942.
Pvt.	LARIN.M.	Les Fusiliers Mont-Royal. R.C.I.C.	19th August 1942.
Pvt.	LAROQUE.A.	Les Fusiliers Mont-Royal. R.C.I.C.	19th August 1942.
Pvt.	LARSH.W.J.	Essex Scottish Regiment. R.C.I.C.	19th August 1942.
Pvt.	LAST.C.R.	South Saskatchewan Regiment R.C.I.C.	19th August 1942.
Pvt.	LAURIE.S	South Saskatchewan Regiment R.C.I.C.	19th August 1942.
L.Cpl.	LAUZON.L.A.	Essex Scottish Regiment. R.C.I.C.	19th August 1942.
Pvt.	LAVER.R.	Royal Regiment of Canada. R.C.I.C.	19th August 1942.
Pvt.	LAVIS.D.	Royal Hamilton Light Infantry. R.C.I.C.	19th August 1942.
Pvt.	LAWRENCE.J.V.	Essex Scottish Regiment. R.C.I.C.	19th August 1942.
Pvt.	LEASK.R.L.	Q.O.Cameron Highlanders of Canada.R.C.I.C.	19th August 1942.
Pvt.	LECLAIR.H.	Les Fusiliers Mont-Royal. R.C.I.C.	19th August 1942.
Pvt.	LECLAIR.M.G.	Royal Regiment of Canada. R.C.I.C.	19th August 1942.
CQ.Sgt.	LEE.A.E.	Royal Regiment of Canada. R.C.I.C.	19th August 1942.
Pvt.	LEE.G.J.	Royal Hamilton Light Infantry. R.C.I.C.	19th August 1942.
Lt.	LEE.P.O.	Essex Scottish Regiment. R.C.I.C.	19th August 1942.
Pvt.	LEESON.R.C.	Royal Hamilton Light Infantry. R.C.I.C.	19th August 1942.
Pvt.	LEIGH.W.M.	Royal Hamilton Light Infantry. R.C.I.C.	19th August 1942.
Pvt.	LENDZIOSZEK.J.K.	Royal Hamilton Light Infantry. R.C.I.C.	19th August 1942.

OPERATION *JUBILEE* - ROLL OF HONOUR

Sgt.	LENNOX.A.	Essex Scottish Regiment. R.C.I.C.	19th August 1942.
Pvt.	LEOPOLD.G.H.	Essex Scottish Regiment. R.C.I.C.	19th August 1942.
Lt.	LEVESQUE.J.J.	Les Fusiliers Mont-Royal. R.C.I.C.	19th August 1942.
Pvt.	LILLYCROP.T.R.	Royal Hamilton Light Infantry. R.C.I.C.	19th August 1942.
Sgt.	LINKLATER.W.B.	Q.O.Cameron Highlanders of Canada.R.C.I.C.	19th August 1942.
L Cpl.	LIPPE.E.	Les Fusiliers Mont-Royal. R.C.I.C.	19th August 1942.
Pvt.	LITTLE.G.E.	Q.O.Cameron Highlanders of Canada.R.C.I.C.	19th August 1942.
Pvt.	LLOYD.L.	Royal Regiment of Canada. R.C.I.C.	19th August 1942.
Pvt.	LLOYD.R.T.	Royal Regiment of Canada. R.C.I.C.	19th August 1942.
Pvt.	LONG.K.G.	Royal Hamilton Light Infantry. R.C.I.C.	19th August 1942.
Pvt.	LOWDEN.N.W.	Royal Regiment of Canada. R.C.I.C.	19th August 1942.
Pvt.	LOZDON.M.	Royal Regiment of Canada. R.C.I.C.	19th August 1942.
Pvt.	LUDGATE.C.G.	Royal Regiment of Canada. R.C.I.C.	19th August 1942.
Pvt.	LUKE.F.	Royal Regiment of Canada. R.C.I.C.	19th August 1942.
Pvt.	MacDONALD.C.	South Saskatchewan Regiment R.C.I.C.	19th August 1942.
Cpl.	MacDONALD.H.A.	Essex Scottish Regiment. R.C.I.C.	19th August 1942.
Pvt.	MacDONALD.W.S.	Royal Regiment of Canada. R.C.I.C.	19th August 1942.
Pvt.	MACK.J.D.	South Saskatchewan Regiment R.C.I.C.	19th August 1942.
Pvt.	MACK.M.W.	Royal Hamilton Light Infantry. R.C.I.C.	19th August 1942.
Pvt.	MacPHERSON.A.D.	Royal Hamilton Light Infantry. R.C.I.C.	19th August 1942.
Pvt.	MADDEN.W.J.	South Saskatchewan Regiment R.C.I.C.	19th August 1942.
Pvt.	MAGDZIASZ.J.	Royal Hamilton Light Infantry. R.C.I.C.	19th August 1942.
Pvt.	MAGNER.P.L.	Royal Hamilton Light Infantry. R.C.I.C.	19th August 1942.
Sgt.	MALONEY.J.E.	Royal Canadian Artillery.	19th August 1942.
Pvt.	MARCEAU.J.E.	Les Fusiliers Mont-Royal. R.C.I.C.	19th August 1942.
Pvt.	MARCOTTE.J.M.	Les Fusiliers Mont-Royal. R.C.I.C.	19th August 1942.
Pvt.	MARGETTS.R.	South Saskatchewan Regiment R.C.I.C.	19th August 1942.
LSgt.	MARLOW.A.H.	Royal Hamilton Light Infantry. R.C.I.C.	19th August 1942.
Pvt.	MARSH.W.J.	Royal Regiment of Canada. R.C.I.C.	19th August 1942.
Sgl.	MARSH.K.L.	Royal Canadian Corps of Signals.	19th August 1942.
Pvt.	MARTEN.L.C.	Q.O.Cameron Highlanders of Canada.R.C.I.C.	19th August 1942.
LSgt.	MARTIN.F.	Royal Hamilton Light Infantry. R.C.I.C.	19th August 1942.
Pvt.	MASON.J.A.	Royal Regiment of Canada. R.C.I.C.	19th August 1942.
Pvt.	MASSE.A.	Les Fusiliers Mont-Royal. R.C.I.C.	19th August 1942.
Sap.	MAVILLE.J.J.	Royal Canadian Engineer's	19th August 1942.
Cpl.	MAVOR.G.R.	South Saskatchewan Regiment R.C.I.C.	19th August 1942.
Pvt.	McANDREW.	Royal Hamilton Light Infantry. R.C.I.C.	19th August 1942.
W.O.II.	McAVOY.J.M.	South Saskatchewan Regiment R.C.I.C.	19th August 1942.
Pvt.	McBRIDE.C.W.	Royal Hamilton Light Infantry. R.C.I.C.	19th August 1942.
Pvt.	McCARROLL.C.K.	Royal Hamilton Light Infantry. R.C.I.C.	19th August 1942.
Pvt.	McCARTHY.J.J.	Royal Regiment of Canada. R.C.I.C.	19th August 1942.
Sap.	McCASLIN.W.H.	Royal Canadian Engineer's	19th August 1942.
Pvt.	McCLEAN.G.F.	Royal Regiment of Canada. R.C.I.C.	19th August 1942.
L Cpl.	McCLEAN.R.W.	Royal Regiment of Canada. R.C.I.C.	19th August 1942.
Pvt.	McCLUSKEY.W.H.	Royal Regiment of Canada. R.C.I.C.	19th August 1942.
Pvt.	McCONNELL.A.J.	Royal Hamilton Light Infantry. R.C.I.C.	19th August 1942.
Pvt.	McCONVILLE.L.A.	Royal Hamilton Light Infantry. R.C.I.C.	19th August 1942.
Pvt.	McCOURT.H.F.	Royal Hamilton Light Infantry. R.C.I.C.	19th August 1942.
Capt.	McCUTCHEON.W.J.	Royal Canadian Artillery.	19th August 1942.

OPERATION *JUBILEE* - ROLL OF HONOUR

Cpl.	McFADDEN.J.A.	Royal Regiment of Canada. R.C.I.C.	19th August 1942.
Pvt.	McFETRIDGE.H.H.	Q.O.Cameron Highlanders of Canada.R.C.I.C.	19th August 1942.
Cpl.	McGHEE.G.W.	Q.O.Cameron Highlanders of Canada.R.C.I.C.	19th August 1942.
Sap.	McGIE.C.	Royal Canadian Engineer's	19th August 1942.
Pvt.	McGLASHAN.N.J.	Royal Regiment of Canada. R.C.I.C.	19th August 1942.
Pvt.	McINTYRE.E.F.	Essex Scottish Regiment. R.C.I.C.	19th August 1942.
Pvt.	McIVOR.T.	Royal Regiment of Canada. R.C.I.C.	19th August 1942.
Lt.	McKELLAR.A.J.	Q.O.Cameron Highlanders of Canada.R.C.I.C.	19th August 1942.
Pvt.	McKEON.P.B.	Essex Scottish Regiment. R.C.I.C.	19th August 1942.
Pvt.	McKINLEY.A.G.	Royal Regiment of Canada. R.C.I.C.	19th August 1942.
Gnr. .	McLEAN.D.	Royal Canadian Artillery.	19th August 1942.
Pvt.	McLEAN.F.	Essex Scottish Regiment. R.C.I.C.	19th August 1942.
Pvt.	McLEOD.R.W.M.	Royal Regiment of Canada. R.C.I.C.	19th August 1942.
Cpl.	McLEOD.T.D.G.	Q.O.Cameron Highlanders of Canada.R.C.I.C.	19th August 1942.
Pvt.	McLISH.R.	Les Fusiliers Mont-Royal. R.C.I.C.	19th August 1942.
Pvt.	McMAHON.E.E.	Q.O.Cameron Highlanders of Canada.R.C.I.C.	19th August 1942.
Lt.	McMANUS.W.W.	Q.O.Cameron Highlanders of Canada.R.C.I.C.	19th August 1942.
Gnr. .	McMULLAN.W.J.	Royal Canadian Artillery.	19th August 1942.
Cpl.	McNAMARA.J.	Royal Hamilton Light Infantry. R.C.I.C.	19th August 1942.
Pvt.	McNERNEY.D.M.	Royal Regiment of Canada. R.C.I.C.	19th August 1942.
Pvt.	McPARLAND.O.	Royal Hamilton Light Infantry. R.C.I.C.	19th August 1942.
Pvt.	MEGSON.R.H.	Royal Hamilton Light Infantry. R.C.I.C.	19th August 1942.
Sgt.	METCALFE.J.R.	Les Fusiliers Mont-Royal. R.C.I.C.	19th August 1942.
Pvt.	MIGHTON.A.	Royal Regiment of Canada. R.C.I.C.	19th August 1942.
Pvt.	MILLAR.S.	Royal Regiment of Canada. R.C.I.C.	25th August 1942.
Pvt.	MILLEN.E.T.	Royal Regiment of Canada. R.C.I.C.	19th August 1942.
Pvt.	MILLER.H.G.	Q.O.Cameron Highlanders of Canada.R.C.I.C.	19th August 1942.
Pvt.	MILLER.R.W.	Royal Hamilton Light Infantry. R.C.I.C.	19th August 1942.
Pvt.	MILLS.J.M.	Royal Regiment of Canada. R.C.I.C.	19th August 1942.
Pvt.	MILOT.J.P.	Les Fusiliers Mont-Royal. R.C.I.C.	19th August 1942.
Pvt.	MINEAU.R.	Les Fusiliers Mont-Royal. R.C.I.C.	19th August 1942.
Pvt.	MINNETT.H.	Royal Hamilton Light Infantry. R.C.I.C.	19th August 1942.
Pvt.	MITICH.G.P.	Royal Regiment of Canada. R.C.I.C.	19th August 1942.
Pvt.	MOFFATT.W.G.	Royal Regiment of Canada. R.C.I.C.	19th August 1942.
Pvt.	MONK.E.E.	Royal Regiment of Canada. R.C.I.C.	19th August 1942.
Pvt.	MONTGOMERY.A.W.	Royal Regiment of Canada. R.C.I.C.	19th August 1942.
Pvt.	MONTGOMERY.R.E.	Royal Regiment of Canada. R.C.I.C.	19th August 1942.
Pvt.	MOORE.M.	Q.O.Cameron Highlanders of Canada.R.C.I.C.	19th August 1942.
Pvt.	MORENCY.P.J.	Essex Scottish Regiment. R.C.I.C.	19th August 1942.
Pvt.	MORLEY.C.L.	Essex Scottish Regiment. R.C.I.C.	19th August 1942.
Pvt.	MORRIS.H.N.	Royal Regiment of Canada. R.C.I.C.	19th August 1942.
Pvt.	MORRISON.H.	Royal Regiment of Canada. R.C.I.C.	19th August 1942.
Pvt.	MORRISON.W.J.	South Saskatchewan Regiment R.C.I.C.	19th August 1942.
Pvt.	MULHOLLAND.J.	Royal Hamilton Light Infantry. R.C.I.C.	19th August 1942.
Pvt.	MURCELL.W.B.	Royal Regiment of Canada. R.C.I.C.	19th August 1942.
Pvt.	MURPHY.R.D.	Essex Scottish Regiment. R.C.I.C.	19th August 1942.
Pvt.	MURRAY.J	Royal Regiment of Canada. R.C.I.C.	19th August 1942.
Sgt.	MURRAY.R.C.	Royal Candian Engineers	19th August 1942.
Pvt.	NAPKEN.J.	Royal Hamilton Light Infantry. R.C.I.C.	19th August 1942.

OPERATION *JUBILEE* - ROLL OF HONOUR

Sgt.	NAYLOR.G.M.	Royal Hamilton Light Infantry. R.C.I.C.	19th August 1942.
Pvt.	NEALE.E.A.	Essex Scottish Regiment. R.C.I.C.	19th August 1942.
LSgt.	NEELANDS.W	Royal Regiment of Canada. R.C.I.C.	26th August 1942.
Cpl.	NESBITT.A.	Les Fusiliers Mont-Royal. R.C.I.C.	19th August 1942.
Pvt.	NEWHOUSE.R.V.	Royal Regiment of Canada. R.C.I.C.	19th August 1942.
Pvt.	NEWTON.R.J.	Royal Hamilton Light Infantry. R.C.I.C.	19th August 1942.
Pvt.	NICKEL. H.R.	Royal Hamilton Light Infantry. R.C.I.C.	19th August 1942.
Pvt.	NORRIS.H.J.	Royal Regiment of Canada. R.C.I.C.	19th August 1942.
Lt.	OAKLEY.R.S.	Royal Regiment of Canada. R.C.I.C.	19th August 1942.
Pvt.	O'KANE.J.G.	Royal Hamilton Light Infantry. R.C.I.C.	19th August 1942.
Sap.	OLIVER.S.G.	Royal Canadian Engineer's	19th August 1942.
Tpr.	OLLIFFE.V.F.	Calgary Regiment, R.C.A.C.	19th August 1942.
Pvt.	O'NEILL.F	Royal Hamilton Light Infantry. R.C.I.C.	19th August 1942.
Sgt.	O'NEILL.J.G.	Royal Hamilton Light Infantry. R.C.I.C.	19th August 1942.
Pvt.	ORPEN.N.G.	Royal Regiment of Canada. R.C.I.C.	19th August 1942.
Pvt.	PARMER.R.F.	Q.O.Cameron Highlanders of Canada.R.C.I.C.	19th August 1942.
Lt.	PARMS.J.C.	Essex Scottish Regiment. R.C.I.C.	19th August 1942.
Pvt.	PAPIC.J.R.	South Saskatchewan Regiment R.C.I.C.	19th August 1942.
Pvt.	PAPILLON.R.	Les Fusiliers Mont-Royal. R.C.I.C.	19th August 1942.
Pvt.	PARENT.E.	Essex Scottish Regiment. R.C.I.C.	19th August 1942.
C.Q.Sgt.	PARENT.N.E.	Les Fusiliers Mont-Royal. R.C.I.C.	19th August 1942.
Pvt.	PATE.J.D.	Essex Scottish Regiment. R.C.I.C.	19th August 1942.
Pvt.	PATERSON.J.A.	Royal Hamilton Light Infantry. R.C.I.C.	19th August 1942.
Pvt.	PATTON.J.J.	Royal Regiment of Canada. R.C.I.C.	19th August 1942.
Sgt.	PEAKS.E.	Royal Regiment of Canada. R.C.I.C.	19th August 1942.
Lt.	PEARCE.J.D.	Royal Regiment of Canada. R.C.I.C.	19th August 1942.
Pvt.	PENDLETON.C.L.	Royal Hamilton Light Infantry. R.C.I.C.	19th August 1942.
Pvt.	PETHERDRIDGE.F.A.	Royal Regiment of Canada. R.C.I.C.	19th August 1942.
Pvt.	PHILLIPS.H.H.	Royal Regiment of Canada. R.C.I.C.	19th August 1942.
Sgt.	PICARD.O.F.	Les Fusiliers Mont-Royal. R.C.I.C.	21st August 1942.
Pvt.	PICKFORD.R.E.	South Saskatchewan Regiment R.C.I.C.	19th August 1942.
Pvt.	PILLEY.H.G.	Royal Hamilton Light Infantry. R.C.I.C.	19th August 1942.
Pvt.	PINKNEY.C.F.	South Saskatchewan Regiment R.C.I.C.	19th August 1942.
Pvt.	PLANTE.O.	Les Fusiliers Mont-Royal. R.C.I.C.	19th August 1942.
Capt.	POAG.H.V.	Royal Hamilton Light Infantry. R.C.I.C.	22nd August 1942.
Pvt.	PODGER.R.	Essex Scottish Regiment. R.C.I.C.	19th August 1942.
Pvt.	POIRIER.J.R.	Les Fusiliers Mont-Royal. R.C.I.C.	19th August 1942.
Pvt.	POITRAS.E.J.	South Saskatchewan Regiment R.C.I.C.	19th August 1942.
Pvt.	POITRAS.G.	Les Fusiliers Mont-Royal. R.C.I.C.	19th August 1942.
Sgt.	POLDEN.A.H.	Royal Regiment of Canada. R.C.I.C.	19th August 1942.
Pvt.	POOLE.E.J.W.	South Saskatchewan Regiment R.C.I.C.	19th August 1942.
Pvt.	POST.C.E.	Essex Scottish Regiment. R.C.I.C.	19th August 1942.
Pvt.	POST.W.E.	Royal Regiment of Canada. R.C.I.C.	19th August 1942.
Cpl.	PRATT.T	Les Fusiliers Mont-Royal. R.C.I.C.	19th August 1942.
Sgt.	PRATT.L.H	Q.O.Cameron Highlanders of Canada.R.C.I.C.	19th August 1942.
Pvt.	PRINE.W	Royal Hamilton Light Infantry. R.C.I.C.	19th August 1942.
Pvt.	PRINGLE.A.M.	Royal Hamilton Light Infantry. R.C.I.C.	19th August 1942.
Pvt.	PROULX.A.	Royal Hamilton Light Infantry. R.C.I.C.	19th August 1942.
Tpr.	PROVIS.C.L.	Calgary Regiment, R.C.A.C.	19th August 1942.

OPERATION *JUBILEE* - ROLL OF HONOUR

Capt.	PURDY.D.G.	Calgary Regiment, R.C.A.C.	19th August 1942.
Pvt.	PURDY.I.L.	Royal Hamilton Light Infantry. R.C.I.C.	19th August 1942.
Pvt.	RAMAGE.W.E.	Royal Regiment of Canada. R.C.I.C.	19th August 1942.
Sgt.	RANKINE.W.L.	Q.O.Cameron Highlanders of Canada.R.C.I.C.	19th August 1942.
Pvt.	RASHOTTE.L.	Les Fusiliers Mont-Royal. R.C.I.C.	19th August 1942.
Pvt.	READSHAW.W.	Les Fusiliers Mont-Royal. R.C.I.C.	19th August 1942.
L Corp	REDWOOD.G.C.	South Saskatchewan Regiment R.C.I.C.	28th August 1942.
Pvt.	"REID,J,H."	Royal Hamilton Light Infantry. R.C.I.C.	19th August 1942.
Pvt.	REID.L.W.	Royal Regiment of Canada. R.C.I.C.	19th August 1942.
Pvt.	REID.T.P.	Royal Hamilton Light Infantry. R.C.I.C.	19th August 1942.
Pvt.	REITH.G.	Royal Regiment of Canada. R.C.I.C.	19th August 1942.
Pvt.	RELF.M.C.	Royal Regiment of Canada. R.C.I.C.	19th August 1942.
Pvt.	RENNIE.J.	Essex Scottish Regiment. R.C.I.C.	19th August 1942.
Pvt.	RENNISON L.N.	Royal Regiment of Canada. R.C.I.C.	19th August 1942.
Pvt.	RHUDA.J.	Royal Regiment of Canada. R.C.I.C.	19th August 1942.
Pvt.	RHYNARD.A.J.	Royal Hamilton Light Infantry. R.C.I.C.	19th August 1942.
Pvt.	RICARD.E.	Royal Regiment of Canada. R.C.I.C.	19th August 1942.
Pvt.	RICHARDS.A.B.	Royal Regiment of Canada. R.C.I.C.	19th August 1942.
Pvt.	RICHARDS.S.	Royal Hamilton Light Infantry. R.C.I.C.	19th August 1942.
Pvt.	RICHARDSON.J.D.	Royal Hamilton Light Infantry. R.C.I.C.	19th August 1942.
Pvt.	RIEDL.V.	Essex Scottish Regiment. R.C.I.C.	19th August 1942.
Pvt.	RIEGER.E.L.	Royal Hamilton Light Infantry. R.C.I.C.	19th August 1942.
Pvt.	RILEY.I.	Royal Regiment of Canada. R.C.I.C.	19th August 1942.
Pvt.	RINKER.D.C.	Essex Scottish Regiment. R.C.I.C.	19th August 1942.
Pvt.	RIVAIT.A.C.	Essex Scottish Regiment. R.C.I.C.	19th August 1942.
Pvt.	RIVAIT.L.M.	Essex Scottish Regiment. R.C.I.C.	19th August 1942.
Pvt.	RIVET.J.W.A.	Les Fusiliers Mont-Royal. R.C.I.C.	19th August 1942.
Pvt.	ROBAR.C.R.	Royal Hamilton Light Infantry. R.C.I.C.	19th August 1942.
Cpl.	ROBERTS.G.W.	Royal Regiment of Canada. R.C.I.C.	19th August 1942.
L Cor	ROBERTS.J.H.	Royal Regiment of Canada. R.C.I.C.	19th August 1942.
Pvt.	ROCHON.R.	Les Fusiliers Mont-Royal. R.C.I.C.	19th August 1942.
Pvt.	ROCHON.A.J.	South Saskatchewan Regiment R.C.I.C.	19th August 1942.
Pvt.	ROLSTON.W.B.	Royal Hamilton Light Infantry. R.C.I.C.	19th August 1942.
Pvt.	ROUSE.D.E.	Royal Regiment of Canada. R.C.I.C.	19th August 1942.
Pvt.	ROWAN.L.	Royal Regiment of Canada. R.C.I.C.	19th August 1942.
Pvt.	ROWE.H.E.	Q.O.Cameron Highlanders of Canada.R.C.I.C.	19th August 1942.
Pvt.	ROY.M.	Les Fusiliers Mont-Royal. R.C.I.C.	19th August 1942.
Pvt.	ROYAN.D.F.	Essex Scottish Regiment. R.C.I.C.	19th August 1942.
Pvt.	RUSHMER.J.S.	South Saskatchewan Regiment R.C.I.C.	19th August 1942.
Pvt.	RUST.W.G.	Royal Hamilton Light Infantry. R.C.I.C.	19th August 1942.
LCorp.	RUTHERFORD.W.A.	Royal Regiment of Canada. R.C.I.C.	19th August 1942.
Pvt.	ST CROIX.W.A.	Q.O.Cameron Highlanders of Canada.R.C.I.C.	19th August 1942.
Pvt.	ST GERMAIN.J.P.	Les Fusiliers Mont-Royal. R.C.I.C.	19th August 1942.
Pvt.	ST LOUIS.M.	Essex Scottish Regiment. R.C.I.C.	19th August 1942.
Pvt.	St PIERRE.T.	Les Fusiliers Mont-Royal. R.C.I.C.	19th August 1942.
Pvt.	SALISBURY.D.F.	Royal Hamilton Light Infantry. R.C.I.C.	19th August 1942.
Cpl.	SALISBURY.W.E.	Royal Hamilton Light Infantry. R.C.I.C.	19th August 1942.
LSgt.	SALMOND.G.	South Saskatchewan Regiment R.C.I.C.	19th August 1942.
Pvt.	SAUTER.E.R.	South Saskatchewan Regiment R.C.I.C.	19th August 1942.

OPERATION *JUBILEE* - ROLL OF HONOUR

Maj.	SAVOY.P.R.	Les Fusiliers Mont-Royal. R.C.I.C.	19th August 1942.
Pvt.	SAWDEN.C.E.	South Saskatchewan Regiment R.C.I.C.	19th August 1942.
Tpr.	SAWERS.W.D.P.	Calgary Regiment, R.C.A.C.	19th August 1942.
Cpl.	SAWYER.S.H.	Royal Regiment of Canada. R.C.I.C.	19th August 1942.
Pvt.	SCHACHT.B.	Q.O.Cameron Highlanders of Canada.R.C.I.C.	19th August 1942.
Maj.	SCHOLFIELD.G.P.	Royal Regiment of Canada. R.C.I.C.	1st September 1942.
LCorp.	SCHOOLEY.C.M.	Essex Scottish Regiment. R.C.I.C.	19th August 1942.
Pvt.	SCOTT.J.H	Royal Regiment of Canada. R.C.I.C.	19th August 1942.
Pvt.	SCOTT.J.L.	Royal Regiment of Canada. R.C.I.C.	19th August 1942.
Pvt.	SCOTT.M.A.J.	Royal Hamilton Light Infantry. R.C.I.C.	19th August 1942.
Pvt.	SEARS.J.	Royal Regiment of Canada. R.C.I.C.	19th August 1942.
Pvt.	SENECAL.R.	Les Fusiliers Mont-Royal. R.C.I.C.	19th August 1942.
Pvt.	SHANK.R.	Royal Regiment of Canada. R.C.I.C.	19th August 1942.
Pvt.	NORTON.T.	South Saskatchewan Regiment R.C.I.C.	19th August 1942.
Pvt.	SHARPE.W.A.	Royal Hamilton Light Infantry. R.C.I.C.	19th August 1942.
Pvt.	SHEPLEY.S.P.	Essex Scottish Regiment. R.C.I.C.	19th August 1942.
Pvt.	SHERRITT.E.W.	Q.O.Cameron Highlanders of Canada.R.C.I.C.	19th August 1942.
Pvt.	SIMARD.A.	Les Fusiliers Mont-Royal. R.C.I.C.	19th August 1942.
LCorp.	SIMPSON.D.H.	Royal Regiment of Canada. R.C.I.C.	19th August 1942.
Capt.	SINCLAIR.G.G.M.I.	Royal Regiment of Canada. R.C.I.C.	19th August 1942.
Pvt.	SINDEN.B.G.	Royal Hamilton Light Infantry. R.C.I.C.	19th August 1942.
Pvt.	SIVERNS.H.	Essex Scottish Regiment. R.C.I.C.	19th August 1942.
Capt.	SKERRETT.G.D.	Royal Hamilton Light Infantry. R.C.I.C.	19th August 1942.
Cpl.	SKROMEDA.S.	Q.O.Cameron Highlanders of Canada.R.C.I.C.	19th August 1942.
LCorp.	SMITH.D.	Royal Regiment of Canada. R.C.I.C.	19th August 1942.
Pvt.	SMITH.E.G.	Royal Regiment of Canada. R.C.I.C.	19th August 1942.
LCorp.	SMITH.F.H.	Royal Hamilton Light Infantry. R.C.I.C.	19th August 1942.
LCorp.	SMITH.G.H.	Royal Hamilton Light Infantry. R.C.I.C.	19th August 1942.
Sap.	SMITH.H.	Royal Canadian Engineers	19th August 1942.
Pvt.	SMITH H.	Royal Hamilton Light Infantry. R.C.I.C.	19th August 1942.
Pvt.	SMITH.J.J.	Royal Regiment of Canada. R.C.I.C.	19th August 1942.
Pvt.	SMITH.L.L.	South Saskatchewan Regiment R.C.I.C.	19th August 1942.
Cpl.	SMITH.R.J.	Royal Regiment of Canada. R.C.I.C.	19th August 1942.
LCorp.	SMITH.R.J.	Royal Regiment of Canada. R.C.I.C.	19th August 1942.
LSgt.	SMITH.S.N.J.	South Saskatchewan Regiment R.C.I.C.	19th August 1942.
Sgl.	SMITH.W.H.	Royal Canadian Corps of Signals.	19th August 1942.
Pvt.	SOMMA.J.	Les Fusiliers Mont-Royal. R.C.I.C.	19th August 1942.
Pvt.	SOMMERVILLE.N.	Royal Hamilton Light Infantry. R.C.I.C.	19th August 1942.
Pvt.	SOUTHWOOD.W.J.	Royal Regiment of Canada. R.C.I.C.	19th August 1942.
Pvt.	SPEED.J.H.	Royal Regiment of Canada. R.C.I.C.	19th August 1942.
Pvt.	SPIKE.H.L.	Royal Regiment of Canada. R.C.I.C.	19th August 1942.
Pvt.	SPRING.H.E.W.	Royal Hamilton Light Infantry. R.C.I.C.	19th August 1942.
Pvt.	SPROULE.C.L.	Royal Regiment of Canada. R.C.I.C.	19th August 1942.
Pvt.	STAINTON.T.	Essex Scottish Regiment. R.C.I.C.	19th August 1942.
Pvt.	STANIUK.P.S.	Royal Hamilton Light Infantry. R.C.I.C.	19th August 1942.
Pvt.	STEELE.J.L.	Royal Regiment of Canada. R.C.I.C.	19th August 1942.
Pvt.	STEERS.J.W.	Essex Scottish Regiment. R.C.I.C.	19th August 1942.
Pvt.	STEVENSON.J.W.	Royal Regiment of Canada. R.C.I.C.	19th August 1942.
Pvt.	STEWART.H.	South Saskatchewan Regiment R.C.I.C.	19th August 1942.

OPERATION *JUBILEE* - ROLL OF HONOUR

LCorp.	STEWART.H.C.	Royal Hamilton Light Infantry. R.C.I.C.	19th August 1942.
Pvt.	STEWART.J.T.	Royal Hamilton Light Infantry. R.C.I.C.	19th August 1942.
Pvt.	STEWART.R.E.	Q.O.Cameron Highlanders of Canada.R.C.I.C.	19th August 1942.
Tpr.	STEWART.W.	Calgary Regiment, R.C.A.C.	19th August 1942.
Pvt.	STILL.H.	Royal Regiment of Canada. R.C.I.C.	19th August 1942.
Pvt.	STOKES.G.H.	Royal Hamilton Light Infantry. R.C.I.C.	19th August 1942.
Gnr. .	STUART.K.M.	Royal Canadian Artillery.	19th August 1942.
Pvt.	SULLIVAN.D.L.	Essex Scottish Regiment. R.C.I.C.	19th August 1942.
Pvt.	SULLIVAN.E.J.	Royal Regiment of Canada. R.C.I.C.	19th August 1942.
Pvt.	SUTTON.S.F.	Q.O.Cameron Highlanders of Canada.R.C.I.C.	19th August 1942.
LCorp.	TAYLOR.A.J.	Essex Scottish Regiment. R.C.I.C.	19th August 1942.
Pvt.	TAYLOR.D.B.	Royal Regiment of Canada. R.C.I.C.	19th August 1942.
Pvt.	TAYLOR.F.G.	Royal Hamilton Light Infantry. R.C.I.C.	19th August 1942.
Pvt.	TAYLOR.J.	Essex Scottish Regiment. R.C.I.C.	19th August 1942.
Pvt.	TAYLOR.R.W.	Royal Hamilton Light Infantry. R.C.I.C.	19th August 1942.
Pvt.	TAYLOR.W.D.	South Saskatchewan Regiment R.C.I.C.	19th August 1942.
Sgt.	TAYLOR.W.G...	Essex Scottish Regiment. R.C.I.C.	19th August 1942.
Cpl.	TEASDALE.G.	Royal Hamilton Light Infantry. R.C.I.C.	19th August 1942.
Pvt.	TEASDALE.P.	Royal Hamilton Light Infantry. R.C.I.C.	19th August 1942.
Sgt.	TEATHER.C.H.	Royal Hamilton Light Infantry. R.C.I.C.	19th August 1942.
Pvt.	TEMPLEMAN.M.	Royal Hamilton Light Infantry. R.C.I.C.	19th August 1942.
Pvt.	THOMPSON.J.	Royal Hamilton Light Infantry. R.C.I.C.	19th August 1942.
Pvt.	THOMPSON.T.	Essex Scottish Regiment. R.C.I.C.	19th August 1942.
Pvt.	THOMSON.N.W.	South Saskatchewan Regiment R.C.I.C.	19th August 1942.
Capt.	THOMSON.W.B.	Royal Regiment of Canada. R.C.I.C.	19th August 1942.
Pvt.	THORNBURY.W.S.P.	Royal Regiment of Canada. R.C.I.C.	19th August 1942.
LCorp.	TREMBLAY.A.	Les Fusiliers Mont-Royal. R.C.I.C.	6th September 1942.
Pvt.	TOWNSEND.J.C.	Royal Regiment of Canada. R.C.I.C.	19th August 1942.
Pvt.	TOWLE.R.K.	Essex Scottish Regiment. R.C.I.C.	19th August 1942.
W.O.11.	TOUGH.A.H.	Calgary Regiment, R.C.A.C.	19th August 1942.
LCorp.	TROMBLEY.L.J.	Essex Scottish Regiment. R.C.I.C.	19th August 1942.
Sgt.	TROMBURG.F.A.	South Saskatchewan Regiment R.C.I.C.	19th August 1942.
Cpl.	TROTTIER.P.J.	Les Fusiliers Mont-Royal. R.C.I.C.	19th August 1942.
Pvt.	TUCK.W.H.	Royal Hamilton Light Infantry. R.C.I.C.	19th August 1942.
Pvt.	TUCKER.H.G.	Royal Regiment of Canada. R.C.I.C.	19th August 1942.
Pvt.	TUCKER.W.J.	Royal Hamilton Light Infantry. R.C.I.C.	19th August 1942.
Pvt.	TULLY.J.B.	Q.O.Cameron Highlanders of Canada.R.C.I.C.	19th August 1942.
Pvt.	TUNSTEAD.W.G.	Royal Regiment of Canada. R.C.I.C.	19th August 1942.
Pvt.	TURMEL.G.	Les Fusiliers Mont-Royal. R.C.I.C.	19th August 1942.
Cpl.	TURNBULL.G.P.	Royal Hamilton Light Infantry. R.C.I.C.	19th August 1942.
Pvt.	TURNER.C.O.	Royal Hamilton Light Infantry. R.C.I.C.	19th August 1942.
Pvt.	TURNER.D.	Royal Hamilton Light Infantry. R.C.I.C.	19th August 1942.
Pvt.	TWYDALE.F.G.	Royal Regiment of Canada. R.C.I.C.	19th August 1942.
Pvt.	TYMAN.D.D.J.	South Saskatchewan Regiment R.C.I.C.	19th August 1942.
Pvt.	TRUDEL.P.A.	Les Fusiliers Mont-Royal. R.C.I.C.	19th August 1942.
Pvt.	TRUMBLEY.R.F.	Royal Hamilton Light Infantry. R.C.I.C.	19th August 1942.
Pvt.	UNDERDAHL.G.T.	South Saskatchewan Regiment R.C.I.C.	19th August 1942.
Pvt.	VALLANCE.D	Essex Scottish Regiment. R.C.I.C.	19th August 1942.

OPERATION *JUBILEE* - ROLL OF HONOUR

Pvt.	VARIN.M.	Les Fusiliers Mont-Royal. R.C.I.C.	19th August 1942.
Pvt.	VAUGHAN.E.R.	Essex Scottish Regiment. R.C.I.C.	19th August 1942.
Pvt.	VERONNEAU.E.	Les Fusiliers Mont-Royal. R.C.I.C.	19th August 1942.
Cpl.	VERREAULT.T.	Les Fusiliers Mont-Royal. R.C.I.C.	19th August 1942.
Gnr. .	VICK.M.R.	Royal Canadian Artillery.	19th August 1942.
Maj.	WALDRON.N.A.	Royal Hamilton Light Infantry. R.C.I.C.	19th August 1942.
Pvt.	WALKER.C.	South Saskatchewan Regiment R.C.I.C.	19th August 1942.
Pvt.	WALKER.J.T.	Royal Regiment of Canada. R.C.I.C.	19th August 1942.
Pvt.	WALKER.J.W.	Royal Hamilton Light Infantry. R.C.I.C.	19th August 1942.
Pvt.	WALKER.R.A.	Royal Regiment of Canada. R.C.I.C.	19th August 1942.
Sgt.	WALKER.R.E.	Royal Regiment of Canada. R.C.I.C.	19th August 1942.
Pvt.	WALKER.W.F.	Essex Scottish Regiment. R.C.I.C.	19th August 1942.
Pvt.	WALL.L.E.	Royal Regiment of Canada. R.C.I.C.	19th August 1942.
Pvt.	WALLACE.R.A.	South Saskatchewan Regiment R.C.I.C.	19th August 1942.
Pvt.	WALMSLEY.J.	Essex Scottish Regiment. R.C.I.C.	19th August 1942.
Pvt.	WALSH.C.B.	Royal Regiment of Canada. R.C.I.C.	19th August 1942.
Pvt.	WALSH.P.J.	Royal Hamilton Light Infantry. R.C.I.C.	19th August 1942.
Lt.	WALTER.W.A.	Royal Regiment of Canada. R.C.I.C.	19th August 1942.
Pvt.	WALTERS.E.R.	Royal Hamilton Light Infantry. R.C.I.C.	19th August 1942.
Pvt.	WARD.R.E.	Royal Regiment of Canada. R.C.I.C.	19th August 1942.
Cpl.	WARDELL.E.H.	Royal Regiment of Canada. R.C.I.C.	19th August 1942.
Pvt.	WARNE.B.V.	Q.O.Cameron Highlanders of Canada.R.C.I.C.	19th August 1942.
Pvt.	WASIK.S.	Royal Regiment of Canada. R.C.I.C.	19th August 1942.
Pvt.	WATSON.H.	Royal Regiment of Canada. R.C.I.C.	19th August 1942.
Cpl.	WEAVER.F.H.	Royal Hamilton Light Infantry. R.C.I.C.	19th August 1942.
Pvt.	WEBB.G.W.E.	Royal Hamilton Light Infantry. R.C.I.C.	19th August 1942.
Lt.	WEDD.W.G.R.	Royal Regiment of Canada. R.C.I.C.	19th August 1942.
LCorp.	WELCH.D.E.	Calgary Regiment, R.C.A.C.	31st August 1942.
Pvt.	WEST.G.C.H.	Q.O.Cameron Highlanders of Canada.R.C.I.C.	19th August 1942.
Sgt.	WHEELER.E.C.S.	Essex Scottish Regiment. R.C.I.C.	19th August 1942.
Pvt.	WHEELER.J.R.	Royal Regiment of Canada. R.C.I.C.	19th August 1942.
Pvt.	WHITE.D.	Essex Scottish Regiment. R.C.I.C.	19th August 1942.
Pvt.	WHITE.J.R.	Royal Regiment of Canada. R.C.I.C.	19th August 1942.
Pvt.	WHYTE.S.J.S.	Royal Hamilton Light Infantry. R.C.I.C.	19th August 1942.
Pvt.	"WICE,R.T."	Royal Hamilton Light Infantry. R.C.I.C.	19th August 1942.
Pvt.	WIGLE.R.	Essex Scottish Regiment. R.C.I.C.	19th August 1942.
Gnr. .	WILKINSON.W.R.	Royal Canadian Artillery.	19th August 1942.
LCorp.	WILLIAMS.J.	South Saskatchewan Regiment R.C.I.C.	19th August 1942.
Pvt.	WILLIAMS.P.A.	Royal Regiment of Canada. R.C.I.C.	19th August 1942.
Sap.	WILLIAMS.S.	Royal Canadian Engineers.	19th August 1942.
Pvt.	WILLIAMSON.M.L.	Royal Regiment of Canada. R.C.I.C.	19th August 1942.
LCorp.	WILLIAMSON.T.E.	Royal Regiment of Canada. R.C.I.C.	19th August 1942.
Maj.	WILLES.J.A.	Essex Scottish Regiment. R.C.I.C.	19th August 1942.
Pvt.	WILSON.D.C.	Q.O.Cameron Highlanders of Canada.R.C.I.C.	19th August 1942.
Pvt.	WILSON.F.F.	Royal Hamilton Light Infantry. R.C.I.C.	19th August 1942.
Pvt.	WINGFIELD.J.H.	Essex Scottish Regiment. R.C.I.C.	19th August 1942.
Pvt.	WINN.J.T	South Saskatchewan Regiment R.C.I.C.	19th August 1942.
Pvt.	WINTERBOTTOM.W.	Essex Scottish Regiment. R.C.I.C.	19th August 1942.
Lt.	WISE.R.A.	Q.O.Cameron Highlanders of Canada.R.C.I.C.	19th August 1942.

OPERATION *JUBILEE* - ROLL OF HONOUR

Pvt.	WITHELL.R.E.	Royal Hamilton Light Infantry. R.C.I.C.	19th August 1942.
Pvt.	WOODBURY.A.C.	Royal Regiment of Canada. R.C.I.C.	19th August 1942.
Pvt.	WOODEY.C.R.	Royal Hamilton Light Infantry. R.C.I.C.	19th August 1942.
Pvt.	WOODLEY.R.D.	Royal Regiment of Canada. R.C.I.C.	19th August 1942.
Lt.	WOOLARD.R.A.	South Saskatchewan Regiment R.C.I.C.	19th August 1942.
Pvt.	WRIGHT.A.	Royal Hamilton Light Infantry. R.C.I.C.	19th August 1942.
Pvt.	WRIGHT.C.K.	Royal Regiment of Canada. R.C.I.C.	19th August 1942.
Lt.	WRIGHT.I.H.V.	Royal Hamilton Light Infantry. R.C.I.C.	19th August 1942.
Pvt.	WYSUKI.V.	Essex Scottish Regiment. R.C.I.C.	19th August 1942.
Pvt.	YASYSZCZUK.W.	Royal Regiment of Canada. R.C.I.C.	19th August 1942.
Pvt.	YOUNG.H.K.	Royal Regiment of Canada. R.C.I.C.	19th August 1942.
Capt.	YOUNG.N.A.T.	Q.O.Cameron Highlanders of Canada.R.C.I.C.	19th August 1942.
Tpr.	ZIMA.M.F.	"Calgary Regiment, R.C.A.C."	19th August 1942.
Pvt.	ZOLYOMY.W.J.	Royal Hamilton Light Infantry. R.C.I.C.	19th August 1942.
Sap.	BISSET.W.N.	Royal Canadian Engineers.	19th August 1942.
Sap.	BREAU.R.A.	Royal Canadian Engineers.	19th August 1942.
Sap.	BROWN.W.A.	Royal Canadian Engineers.	19th August 1942.
Sap.	CHARBOTTE.P.	Royal Canadian Engineers.	19th August 1942.
LCpl.	HALL.A.H.	Royal Canadian Engineers.	19th August 1942.
LCol.	McTAVISH.G.H.	Royal Canadian Engineers.	19th August 1942.
Sap.	RAMSAY.J.	Royal Canadian Engineers.	19th August 1942.
Cpl.	RUSSELL.T.D.	Royal Canadian Engineers.	19th August 1942.
Sap.	SHARP.C.J.	Royal Canadian Engineers.	19th August 1942.
Sap.	SHOVA.E.	Royal Canadian Engineers.	19th August 1942.
Pvt.	DAVIDSON.R.D.	Essex Scottish Regiment. R.C.I.C.	19th August 1942.
Sap.	BERGEY.O.L.	Royal Canadian Engineers.	19th August 1942.
Sap.	BOCKUS.L.E.	Royal Canadian Engineers.	19th August 1942.
Sap.	HODSON.C.	Royal Canadian Engineers.	19th August 1942.

BRITISH SOLDIERS LOST.

Pvt.	Broster,.John.	Cheshire Regiment,	No.3.Commando.	19th August 1942.
Pvt.	Broadbent, Fred, S.	Royal Army Med Corps.	No.3.Commando.	19th August 1942.
Pvt.	Bryan,John, R.	Duke of Cornwall's Light Infantry.		19th August 1942.
Gnr.	Cooper, George,W.	Royal Artillery,	No.3.Commando.	19th August 1942.
LCpl.	Craggs, William,	Ley 2nd Bn.Rifle Brigade.		19th August 1942.
Pvt.	Garthwaite,William, O.	Loyal Reg, (N. Lancashire)	No.4.Commando	19th August 1942.
Pvt.	Gooch, Frederick, M,	East Surrey Regiment.	No.4.Commando.	19th August 1942.
Pvt.	Fisher, Douglas, M,	Gordon Highlanders.	No.3.Commando.	19th August 1942.
Pvt.	Harding,.Ernest, F.	Devonshire Regiment.	No.3.Commando.	19th August 1942.
LCpl.	Harding,.Richard.	Royal Armoured Corps.	No.3.Commando.	19th August 1942.
LCpl.	Heckman,.Edward, P.	Royal Berkshire Regiment.	No.4.Commando.	19th August 1942.
LCpl.	Mills, Alexander.	South Lancashire Regiment.	No.4.Commando.	19th August 1942.
LSgt.	Mill,s.Joseph,W.	Beds & Herts Regiment.	No.3.Commando	19th August 1942.
Pvt.	Oppelt, Gustav.	93.Coy.Pioneer Corps.		19th August 1942.
Pvt.	Rhodes,.Francis.M.	Beds & Herts Regiment.	No.3.Commando	19th August 1942.
Pvt.	Sutton,.George.H.	East Yorkshire Regiment.	No.4.Commando.	19th August 1942.
Capt.	Thomas,.James.H.	Royal Artillery,	No.3.Commando.	19th August 1942.
Gnr.	Wall,.William.	Royal Artillery,	No.3.Commando.	19th August 1942.
Maj.	Wyatt,.David.A.	Royal Engineers.		19th August 1942.

OPERATION *JUBILEE* - ROLL OF HONOUR

ROYAL AIR FORCE CREWS KILLED.

Rank	Name	Nationality.	Aircraft.	Crew	
Sq Ldr.	BERRY.A.E.	New Zealand.	Hurricane.	Pilot.	19th Aug 1942.
Sgt.	BANKS. S.D.	Canadian.	Hurricane.	Pilot.	19th Aug 1942.
P/Offr.	WOODLAND.C.L.	British.	Blenheim.	Pilot.	19th Aug 1942.
Sgt.	BOYD.A.S.	Irish.	Blenheim.	Observer.	19th Aug 1942.
Sgt.	NEVILLE.H.G.	Australian	Blenheim.	Air/Gunner	19th Aug 1942.
Sgt.	BLORE.E.A.	British.	Spitfire.	Pilot.	19th Aug 1942.
Fl/Lt.	DAWSON.G.N.	British.	Mustang.	Pilot.	19th Aug 1942.
Fl/Lt.	KENNEDY.		Mustang.	Pilot.	19th Aug 1942.
Sgt.	CLIFF.G.D.M.	British.	Mustang.	Pilot.	19th Aug 1942.
Fl/Lt.	CONNOLLY.H.	British.	Hurricane.	Pilot.	19th Aug 1942.
Sq Ldr.	HYDE.G.C.	British.	Spitfire.	Pilot.	19th Aug 1942.
F/Sgt.	WIK.H.	Canadian.	Hurricane.	Pilot.	19th Aug 1942.
Sgt.	McCUAIG.E.N.	Scottish.	Spitfire.	Pilot.	19th Aug 1942.
P/Offr.	STEWART.J.K.	Rhodesian	Spitfire.	Pilot.	19th Aug 1942.
Sgt.	LYONS.R.	Canadian.	Spitfire.	Pilot.	19th Aug 1942.
Lt	NISSEN. V.R.E.	South African.	Spitfire.	Pilot.	19th Aug 1942.
P/Offr.	WALTOS.A.S.M.	Polish	Hurricane.	Pilot.	19th Aug 1942.
Sgt.	GIBSON.R.	British.	Hurricane.	Pilot.	19th Aug 1942.
WO	BEACH.C.A.	Canadian.	Boston.	Pilot.	19th Aug 1942.
Sgt.	HINDLE. D.F.J.		Boston.	Observer.	19th Aug 1942.
Sgt.	HINDLEY.E.J	British.	Spitfire.	Pilot.	19th Aug 1942.
P/Offr.	TAYLOR.J.T.	American.	Spitfire.	Pilot.	19th Aug 1942.
F/Offr.	JONES.H.G.	Welsh.	Spitfire.	Pilot.	19th Aug 1942.
Sgt.	JONSSEN.S.G.	Norwegian	Spitfire.	Pilot.	19th Aug 1942.
Sgt.	UTTING.A.W.	British.	Spitfire.	Pilot.	19th Aug 1942.
Sq Ldr.	FAYOLLE.E.M.L.	French.	Hurricane.	Pilot.	19th Aug 1942.
Sgt.	JAMES.C.F.	British.	Hurricane.	Pilot.	19th Aug 1942.
P/Offr.	du FRETAY.M.H.	French.	Hurricane.	Pilot.	19th Aug 1942.
Fl/Lt.	McWILLIAM.O.G.E.		Boston.	Passenger	19th Aug 1942.
P/Offr.	WALTERS.L.J.		Boston.	Air/Gunner	19th Aug 1942.
P/Offr.	CORRIGAN.R.J.	American.	Boston.	Pilot.	19th Aug 1942.
F/Sgt.	OSSELTON.W.	British.	Boston.	Air/Gunner	19th Aug 1942.
Fl/Lt.	STRONG.P.D.		Spitfire.	Pilot.	19th Aug 1942.
Sgt.	WALKER.K.G.	British.	Spitfire.	Pilot.	19th Aug 1942.
P/Offr.	CRUICKSHANK.J.R.		Mustang.	Pilot.	19th Aug 1942.
F/Offr.	GOMPERTZ.P.A.L.	British.	Mustang.	Pilot.	19th Aug 1942.
Fl/Lt.	BENNETTE.G.R.	British.	Hurricane.	Pilot.	19th Aug 1942.
P/Offr.	BARTON.J.E.	New Zealand.	Hurricane.	Pilot.	19th Aug 1942.
P/Offr.	SCOTT.A.E.	British.	Hurricane.	Pilot.	19th Aug 1942.
P/Offr.	SMITHYSON.W.S.		Typhoon.	Pilot.	19th Aug 1942.
Fl/Lt.	DAWSON.R.H.L.	Rhodesian	Typhoon.	Pilot.	19th Aug 1942.
P/Offr.	DAMM.A.	Polish	Spitfire.	Pilot.	19th Aug 1942.
Lt	WIGHT.R.G.	American.	Spitfire.	Pilot.	19th Aug 1942.
Lt	COLLINS	American.	Spitfire.	Pilot.	19th Aug 1942.
Adt	DARBIN.R.G.	French.	Spitfire.	Pilot.	19th Aug 1942.
P/Offr.	BURLINGHAM. D.G.	Canadian.	Mustang.	Pilot.	19th Aug 1942.
Sgt.	BUCKLEY.M.H.	Canadian.	Spitfire.	Pilot.	19th Aug 1942.

Operation *Jubilee* - Roll of Honour

P/Offr.	GARDINER.J.E.	Canadian.	Spitfire.	Pilot.	19th Aug 1942.
P/Offr.	WALKER.L.A.	Canadian.	Spitfire.	Pilot.	19th Aug 1942.
P/Offr.	MONCHIER.N.	Canadian.	Spitfire.	Pilot.	19th Aug 1942.
P/Offr.	EAKINS.P.R.	Canadian.	Spitfire.	Pilot.	19th Aug 1942.
P/Offr.	LINTON.D.	Canadian.	Spitfire.	Pilot.	19th Aug 1942.
P/Offr.	BROOKHOUSE.J.N.	Canadian.	Spitfire.	Pilot.	19th Aug 1942.
Sgt.	LEE.A		Spitfire.	Pilot.	19th Aug 1942.
Fl/Lt.	POOLE.P.D.		Spitfire.	Pilot.	19th Aug 1942.
Sgt.	LEECH.J.G.		Spitfire.	Pilot.	19th Aug 1942.
F/Sgt.	VILBOUX.A.P.F.	French.	Spitfire.	Pilot.	19th Aug 1942.
Sgt.	JOHNSON.W.		Blenheim.	Observer.	19th Aug 1942.
F/Sgt.	GIFKINS.G.R.		Blenheim.	Air/Gunner	19th Aug 1942.
Sgt.	COLDRAY.N.W.J.	Rhodesian	Spitfire.	Pilot.	19th Aug 1942.
W.Comdr	SKINNER.S.H.	90210	R.A.F.Observer		19th Aug 1942.

ROYAL AIR FORCE, AIR-SEA RESCUE CREWS LOST

F/Offr.	HILL.J.R.	108368	H.S.L.122.	Skipper.	19th Aug 1942.	961.Sqn.
Sgt.	OSBOURNE.F.	1104514	H.S.L.122.	M.B.C.	19th Aug 1942.	961.Sqn.
Cpl.	APPLEBY.R.A.	1375497	H.S.L.122.	M.B.C.	19th Aug 1942.	961.Sqn.
L.A.C.	DENNIS.D.B.	1383547	H.S.L.122.	M.B.C.	19th Aug 1942.	961.Sqn.
L.A.C.	GOOD.H.K.	1458804	H.S.L.122.	M.B.C.	19th Aug 1942.	961.Sqn.
L.A.C.	MOSS.R.J.	1465905	H.S.L.122.	M.B.C.	19th Aug 1942.	961.Sqn.
L.A.C.	WILKINS.F.S.	1459634	H.S.L.123.	M.B.C.	19th Aug 1942.	961.Sqn.
L.A.C.	KRAFT.C.W.	1358992	H.S.L.123.	W/Om.	19th Aug 1942.	961.Sqn.
F/Offr.	BROAD.R.	110142	H.S.L.147.	Skipper.	19th Aug 1942.	961.Sqn.
Sgt.	STEPHENS.J.S.	630346	H.S.L.147.	M.B.C.	19th Aug 1942.	961.Sqn.
L.A.C.	BAMBRIDGE.E.H.	1383840	H.S.L.147.	M.B.C.	19th Aug 1942.	961.Sqn.
L.A.C.	CURTISS.F.	1453926	H.S.L.147.	M.B.C.	19th Aug 1942.	961.Sqn.
L.A.C.	SUTTON.A.W.	1054416	H.S.L.147.	N/ORD	19th Aug 1942.	961.Sqn.
L.A.C.	STEPHENSON.R.F.	1516941	H.S.L.147.	M.B.C.	19th Aug 1942.	961.Sqn.

H.M.S.BERKLEY. L.17.DIEPPE. 19th AUGUST 1942.

Lt, R.N.	YORK.JAMES.J.S.	COM.OFFICER.
AS, R.N.	ADAMS.JOHN.	PSSX 262379.
OS, R.N.	ADAMS.STEPHEN.	JX 295058.
STOKER. R.N.	ANDREWS.	PKX 100610.
TEL.RN.	ARCHARD.PATRICK.	DJX 215196.
O/TEL.RN.	ARSCOTT.JOHN.C.	PJX 263793.
E.R.A.RN.	BAILEY.HENRY T.	PJX 65256.
OS, R.N.	BETHELL.RONALD.	PJX 274697.
SUB/LT. RNVR.	BINCH.JOHN.H.	
CODER.RN.	BIRKETT. HOWARD.J.	PJX 199620.
AS, R.N.	BLACKBURN.HARVEY.	PJX 170090.
AS, R.N.	BONLEY. WILFRED.A.	PJX 203399.
P.O., R.N.	BOOTHROYD.GEORGE.T.	PJ 112416.
AS, R.N.	BOYD.GUY.C.	PJX 235998.
CH/ E.R.A. R.N.	BRADING.BERTRAM.S.	PM 36662.

OPERATION *JUBILEE* - ROLL OF HONOUR

OS, R.N.	BRADLEY.WILLIAM.	PJX 291764.	
O/TEL.RN.	BRISCOE.HAROLD.V.	PJX 282457.	
P.O., R.N.	BROOK.HARRY.	PJX 135236.	
O/SIG.RN.	BROWN HERBERT.	PJX 277013.	
AS, R.N.	BURBERRY. LEWIS.G.	PJX 261293.	
STOKER. R.N.	BURTON.CYRIL.R.	PKX 100604.	
ORD/ART.R.N.	BUSS.REGINALD.G.	PMX 45600.	
TEL.RN.	CARLISLE.WILLIAM.R.	PJX 159762.	
O/SIG.RN.	CHESHIRE.TREVOR.S.	PJX 260148.	
PO/STO.R.N	CLAIR.GEORGE.H.W.	PK 59599.	
L/SEA.R.N	CLARK.RONALD.	PSSX 21887.	
OS, R.N.	CLARKE.REGINALD.G.	PJX 264514.	
ASST/STWD.R.N.	COOPER.CHARLES.R.	PLX 25389.	DIED. 19/08/42.
AS, R.N.	COX.CHARLES.R.	PSSX 34048.	
STOKER. R.N.	COX.JOHN.O.B.	PKX 115752.	DIED. 19/08/42.
L/STO.R.N.	CREMMINS.MARTIN.	PK 58536.	
AS, R.N.	DICKSON.CHARLES.	PJX 109474.	
PO/STO.R.N	DIVER.FREDERICK.	PKX 75867.	
OS, R.N.	DONNER. FREDERICK.A.	PJX 273509.	
OS, R.N.	DOOTSON.OWEN.	PJX 250156.	
L/STWD.R.N.	DOWNER.ALBERT.E.	PL 12179.	
OS, R.N.	DRONSFIELD.CYRIL.	PJX 282130.	
OS, R.N.	DUKE.GEOFFREY.H.	PJX 274094.	
STOKER. R.N.	EDWARDS.WALTER.R.	PKX 100608.	
AS, R.N.	EGGLETON.THOMAS.A.J.	PSSX 33995.	
C.P.O./STO.R.N.	ELLIS.ALWYN.P.	PK 55122.	
AS, R.N.	EVANS.F.R.	CKX 102811.	
AS, R.N.	EVANS.THOMAS.R.	PJX 171396.	
AS, R.N.	FOOTITT.WILLIAM.	PJX 203592.	
AS, R.N.	FORGIE.PETER.F.	PSSX 36148.	
STOKER. R.N.	FORRESTER.WALTER.E.	PKX 128623.	
OS, R.N.	FUNNELL.GEORGE.	PJX 324151.	
STOKER. R.N.	FUNNELL.WALTER.H.	PKX 101469.	
AS, R.N.	GEORGE.ARCHIE.F.	PJX 215549.	DIED. 19/08/42.
OS, R.A.N.V.R.	GILLING.DOUGLAS.G.	SV 83.	
PO/STO.R.N	GORSUCH.HARRY.B.	PK 61963.	
STOKER. R.N.	GRAY.JAMES.	PKX 108864.	
P.O., R.N.	GROOM.DAVID.L.G.	PJX 128432.	
STOKER. R.N.	GROSS.HENRY.G.	PKX 100599.	
PO/TEL.R.N.	HALL.WILLIAM.	PJ 69024.	
C.P.O.R.N.	HALLETT.FREDERICK.C.	PJ 33846.	
L/MECH.R.N.	HALLIDAY. ROBERT.J.	LDX 4019.	
L/STOKER.R.N.	HANNAM.JOSEPH.R.	PKX 94143.	
SUPP/ASST.R.N.	HARE.THOMAS.	PMX 65087.	WND.
AS, R.N.	HARRINGTON.ALFRED.W.	PSSX 17798.	
STOKER. R.N.	HARRISON.FREDERICK.C.C.	PKX 115757	
AS, R.N.	HARRISON.THOMAS.	PSSX 18043.	
STOKER. R.N.	HASTIE.JAMES.	PKX 131920.	DIED. 19/08/42.
STOKER. R.N.	HATLEY.GEORGE.	PKX 128536.	

OPERATION *JUBILEE* - ROLL OF HONOUR

STOKER. R.N.	HAYLETT.GEORGE.E.	PKX 128035.	DIED. 19/08/42.
AS, R.N.	HAYNES.FRANCES.C.	PJX 221913.	
OS, R.N.	HEANEY.ALEXANDER.	PJX 302036.	
LS, R.N.	HENDERSON.ALBERT.	PX 103988.	
AS, R.N.	HEWETT. KENNETH.C.	PJX 171291.	
AS, R.N.	HIGSON.GILES.	PJX 171188.	
OS, R.N.	HILL.KENNETH.D.	PJX 322010.	
STOKER. R.N.	HODGE.GEORGE.J.	PKX 115762.	
OS, R.N.	HODGES.HAROLD.E.	PJX 273554.	
OS, R.N.	HOOPER.STANLEY.	PJX 252808.	
STOKER. R.N.	HORTON.WILLIAM.	PKX 144499.	
PO/STR.R.N.	HUGHES.GEORGE.	PKX 84265.	
PO/STR.R.N.	HUMPHREY.ROLAND.J.F.	PK 61480.	
AS, R.N.	HUNT.SYDNEY.W.	PJX 152739.	
AS, R.N.	JACKSON.LESLIE.R.	PJX 150211.	
P.O., R.N.	JAMES.HENRY.G.	PL 12827.	
L/WRITER.R.N.	JAY.ALLAN.C.	CMX 86614.	
SBA.R.N.	JONES.THOMAS.A.	PMX 81753.	
L/STOKER.R.N.	JONES.WILLIAM.F.	PKX 92604.	
STOKER. R.N.	KEW.GEORGE.J.	PKX 129909.	
SIG.R.N.	KNIGHT.JEFFREY. H.	PJX226765.	
AS, R.N.	LEASON.REGINALD.A.	PJX 262782.	
PO/SUPPLY.R.N.	LEGG.MATTHEW.W.R.	PMX 45452.	
AS, R.N.	LEGGETT.ROBERT.L.	DJX 204406.	
OS, R.N.	LEWIS.BERNARD.L.	PJX 307241.	
SUB/LT. RNVR.	LOWCOCK.RICHARD.L.(GNR)		
LS, R.N.	LOWE.THOMAS.	PJ 23400.	DIED. 19/08/42.
LS, R.N.	MANSFIELD.HUGH.E.	PJ 108888.	
P.O., R.N.	MARCHANT.BASIL. V.B.	PJX 139675.	
AS, R.N.	MARSHALL.LAURENCE.	PJX 183514.	DIED. 19/08/42.
AS, R.N.	MARSHALL.WILLIAM.L.	PJX 146194.	
OS, R.N.	MARTIN.GEORGE.R.	PJX 275253.	
AS, R.N.	MARTIN.WALTER.J.	PJ 83878.	DIED. 19/08/42.
OS.R.N.R.	MASSON GEORGE. D.	X 17933A.	
STWD.R.N.	MATTINSON.ROBERT.W.	PLX 27889.	
OS, R.N.	MILLS.JOHN	PJX 323197.	
OS. .R.N.	MINTO.PATRICK.	PJX 325786.	
L/COOK.(S) R.N.	MITCHARD LEONARD.F.	PMX 51915.	DIED. 19/08/42.
CANTEEN MNGR.	MITCHELL.F.W.H.		
L/COOK.R.N.	MITCHELL.KENNETH.	PMX 57731.	
P.O., R.N.	MOODY.ALBERT.T.	PJ 114466.	DIED. 19/08/42.
OS. .R.N.	MORRIS.JOSEPH.	PJX 273819.	
AS, R.N.	MOULAND.HARRY.J.	CJX 230253.	
E.R.A.RN.	McCANN.JAMES.F.	PMX 78676.	
STOKER. R.N.	McCULLOCH.ERNEST.	PK 66996.	
STOKER. R.N.	McIVOR.ALEXANDER.	PK 47266.	
1ST LT.R.N.	McLAUGHLAN.IAN.D.		
L/WRITER.R.N.	McMURDO. ROBERT.	CMX 96928.	
LS, R.N.	NEIGHBOUR.SIDNEY.G.	PJ 95936.	

OPERATION *JUBILEE* - ROLL OF HONOUR

AS, R.N.	NELSON.HUGH.A.	PSSX 32355.	
AS, R.N.	NEWELL.JACOB.E.	PJX 188924.	
LS, R.N.	NEWTON.IVOR.W.	PJX 144876.	
AS, R.N.	NIGHTINGDALE.THOMAS.D.	PSSX 21128.	
L/STOKER.R.N.	NORRIS.GEORGE.U.	PKX 83492.	
YEO/SIG. R.N.	NORTON.ALEXANDER.	PJ 112797.	
ELECT/ART. R.N.	O'NEILL.EDMUND.	PMX 46684.	
AS, R.N.	OLIVER.FRANK.	PJX 176080.	
AS, R.N.	OSBORNE.WILLIAM.A.E.	PJX 182627.	
PO/COOK.R.N.	PAYNE.JOHN.H.	PMX 48043.	
AS, R.N.	PEAR.LAWRENCE.J.	PJX 188871.	
AS, R.N.	PEASE.ARTHUR.W.J.G.	PJX 182632.	DIED. 19/08/42.
STOKER. R.N.	PHELPS. ERNEST.G	PKX 101469.	
AS, R.N.	PHILLIPS.SAMUEL.L.	PJX 178463.	
O/TEL.R.N.	PHILPOTT.WILLIAM.H.	PJX 308516.	
STOKER. R.N.	PIGGOTT.ALFRED.H.	PKX 128646.	
LS, R.N.	POTTER.ALBERT.E.	DJX 131083.	
AS, R.N.	PRESHAW.WILLIAM.	PJX 173969.	
CODER.R.N.	PRESTON.RALPH.W.	PJX 199652.	
AS, R.N.	PROTHEROE.WILLIAM.	PJX 174125.	
AS, R.N.	RHODEN MAURICE.	PJX 172697.	
AS, R.N.	RIDDLES.ARTHUR.	PJ 45602.	
AS, R.N.	RIDEOUT. HERBERT.E.	PJ 31734.	
AS, R.N.	RISHMAN. SIDNEY.R.	PJX 170079.	WND.
O/TEL.R.N.	ROBINS.CHARLES.F.	PJX 258687.	
AS, R.N.	ROBSON.EDWARD.H.	PJX 176761.	
STOKER. R.N.	ROSE.ARTHUR.C.	PKX 101363.	
AS, R.N.	RUSSELL.SYDNEY.E.J.	PJX 273459.	
AS, R.N.	RYDER.LESLIE.	PJX 275628.	
OS. .R.N.	SHAND.WILLIAM.J.S.	PJX 275818.	
LS, R.N.	SIMPSON.STANLEY.E.C.	PSSX 17263.	
OS. .R.N. .	SKIPTON.EDWIN.W.	PJX 282129.	
AS, R.N.	SMITH.DOUGLAS.G.	PJX 265534.	DIED. 19/08/42.
E.R.A.RN.	SMITH.WILFRED.V.B.	PMX 52411.	
OS. .R.N.	SNEDDON.WILLIAM.	PJX 321841.	
LS, R.N.	SOPP.RICHARD.J.	PSSX 20866.	
AS, R.N.	SPAIN.THOMAS.H.	PJX 26553.?.	
SHIPWT.R.N.	STEPHENS.ERNEST.E.	PM 34620.	
L/COOK(S) R.N.	STONE.FREDERICK.	PMX 60573.	DIED. 19/08/42.
LT/SURG.R.N.V.R.	STOTT.DONALD.V.		WND.
AS, R.N.	SULLIVAN.THOMAS.	PJX 217655.	
L/STOKER.R.N.	TAYLOR.DONALD.E.	PKX 88887.	
OS. .R.N.	TAYLOR.FRANK.	PJX 276196.	
AS, R.N.	TAYLOR.REGINALD.V.	PJX 176515.	
OS. .R.N.	THOMAS.HAROLD.H.	PJX 323638.	DIED. 19/08/42.
LT.NAV.R.N.	TOWNLEY.JOHN.M.		
OS. .R.N.	TUCK.STANLEY.F.	PJX 132630.	
P.O.STR.R.N.	TUTTON.HERBERT.F.	PK 66243.	DIED. 19/08/42.
OS. .R.N.	VALLOM.FREDERICK.T.	PJX 296069.	

OPERATION *JUBILEE* - ROLL OF HONOUR

OS. .R.N.	VENABLES.FREDERICK.R.	PJX 250165.
AS, R.N.	WADE.ERIC.	PJX 235878.
AS, R.N.	WARD.ERIC.J.	PJX 199249.
L/S.ASST.R.N.	WELCH.PERCIVAL.	PMX 53450.
SIG.R.N.	WILKINS.FREDERICK.R.	PSSX 33358.
AS, R.N.	WILLIAMS.STUART.A.	PJX 182235.
E.R.A.RN.	WITT. WILLIAM.E.J.	PMX58820.
STOKER. R.N.	WRIGHT.HENRY.	PKX 115686.

ROLL OF HONOUR. H.M.S.BERKLEY L17.DIEPPE

ASST/STWD.R.N.	COOPER.CHARLES.R.	PL/X 25389	19th Aug 1942.
STOKER.R.N.	COX. JOHN O.	PK/X 116752.	19th Aug 1942.
AS, R.N.	GEORGE. A. F.	PJ/X 215549.	19th Aug 1942.
STOKER.R.N.	HASTIE. JAMES.	PK/X 131920.	19th Aug 1942.
STOKER.R.N.	HAYLETT. GEORGE E.	PK/X.128035.	19th Aug 1942.
L/SEAMAN. R.N.	LOWE.THOMAS.	PJ 23400.	19th Aug 1942.
AS, R.N.	MARSHALL.LAURENCE.	PJ/X 183514.	19th Aug 1942.
AS, R.N.	MARTIN.WALTER G.	PJ 83878.	19th Aug 1942.
L/COOK R.N.	MITCHARD.LEONARD F.	PM/X 51915.	19th Aug 1942.
P.O..R.N.	MOODY.ALBERT G.	PJ 114466.	19th Aug 1942.
AS, R.N.	PEASE.ARTHUR W.	PJ/X 182632.	19th Aug 1942.
AS, R.N.	SMITH.DOUGLAS G.	PJ/X 265534.	19th Aug 1942.
COOK(S) R.N.	STONE.FREDERICK.	PM/X 60573.	19th Aug 1942.
OS	THOMAS.HAROLD H.	PJ/X 323638.	19th Aug 1942.
P/Offr.STR.R.N.	TUTTON.HERBERT F.	PK 66243.	19th Aug 1942.

NAVY PERSONNEL BURIED IN DIEPPE.

Sub Lt..	WINNICOTT, ROBERT R.		19th Aug 1942.
OS.	CARROLL, WILLIAM P,	P/JX 322780	19th Aug 1942.
STOKER 2nd CL.	HOLT, HECTOR.	P/KX 139093.	19th Aug 1942.
O TELEG.	NORRINGTON, PETER A.	P/JX 323499.	19th Aug 1942.
SIGNALMAN.	WESTERN, KENNETH, J.	D/JX 233250.	19th Aug 1942.
SICK BERTH ATT.	DICKINSON, JOSEPH V.H.	D/MX 74834.	19th Aug 1942.
A.S.	PHEBY, RALPH F.	P/JX 223930.	19th Aug 1942.
O.S.	FLANAGAN, GEORGE.	P/JX 296319.	19th Aug 1942.
L.S.	BUTLER, HUGH.	P/JX 156656	19th Aug 1942.
L.S.	RELPH, JAMES.	P/JX 153618.	19th Aug 1942.

R.A.F. LAUNCHES ON THE DIEPPE RAID.

H.S.L.s. 122.123.147.186.Dover.
H.S.L.s. 104.106.116.117.177.Newhaven.
H.S.L.s. 120.127.Ramsgate.

Operation *Jubilee* - Roll of Honour

ROYAL MARINES COMMANDOS KILLED.

LIEUTENANT.	OVER.DERICK.G.		19th Aug 1942.
RM CDO.CPL.	EVERALL.HENRY.J.	PLY/X2081.	19th Aug 1942.
RM.CDO.M.	GOTTS.ERIC.W.	PO/X2274.	19th Aug 1942.
RM.CDO.M.	POWER.WALLACE.W.	CH/X3243.	19th Aug 1942.
RM.CDO.M.	RIDDLE.ALBERT.H.I.	PO/3021.	19th Aug 1942.
RM.CDO.SGT.	BEESLEY.JACK.	CH/X844.	19th Aug 1942.

VESSELS INVOLVED IN OPERATIONS.

H.M.S. Albrighton.	H.M.S. Alresford.	H.M.S. Bangor.
H.M.S. Berkeley.	H.M.S. Blackpool.	H.M.S. Bleakdale.
H.M.S. Dlyth.	H.M.S. Bridlington.	H.M.S. Bridport.
H.M.S. Brocklesby.	H.M.S. Calpe.	H.M.S. Clacton.
H.M.S. Duke of Wellington.	H.M.S. Eastbourne.	H.M.S. Felixstowe.
H.M.S. Fernie.	H.M.S. Garth.	H.M.S. Glengyle.
H.M.S. Ilfracombe.	H.M.S. Invicta.	H.M.S. Locust.
H.M.S. Polruan.	H.M.S. Prince Charles.	H.M.S. Prince Leopold.
H.M.S Prince Albert.	H.M.S. Princess Astrid.	H.M.S. Princess Beatrix.
H.M.S. Queen Emma.	H.M.S. Rhyl.	H.M.S Sidmouth.
H.M.S. Sidmouth.	H.M.S Stornoway.	H.M.S. Tenby.

M.L.s. 114, 120, 123, 171, 187, 189, 190, 193, 194, 208, 214, 230, 246, 291, 292,
M.L.s. 309, 343, 344, 346, 191
M.G.B.s 50, 51, 312, 315, 316, 317, 320, 323, 326, 52.57.321.
S.G.B.s. 5, 6, 8, 9.

LANDING CRAFT LOST IN THE LANDINGS.

L.C.A.s No.37. 52. 92. 94. 97. 102. 192. 209. 214. 215. 237. 247. 251. 262. 284. 314. 317.
L.C.F.s Mk2.L.C.M. No.2.
L.C.M.s. Mk1. L.C.M. No.56.
L.C.P.s.(L) No.42. 45. 81. 157. 164. 174. 210. 212.
L.C.S.s (M) No.9.
L.C.T.s. No. 121. 124. 126. 145. 159.

LANDING CRAFT TAKING PART.

L.C.P.(L) 85.42.81.7.1.15.80.86.87.95.118.128.145.19.88.94.119.124.125.129.147.156.45.
157.164.174.210.212.
L.C.F.(L) 1.2.3.4.5.6.
L.C.T.s
145.127.159.126.121.163.124.125.165.166.169.305.304.303.302.306.308.376.361.309.310.360.307.318.3
25.
L.C.S. 25.8.9.31.21.
L.C.M. 56.
L.C.A.s
208.209.170.521.315.198.185.187.188.176.197.186.215.262.317.251.214.250.314.195.212.175.192.174.1
73.199.172.53.28.37.52.92.94.97.102.237.247.284.

Air Support from RAF Friston

RAF Friston aerodrome, near Seaford, had a lesser role initially in the Second World War. During the Operation *Jubilee* it was the closest Allied airfield to the Dieppe shores. As the actions developed the cliff-top airfield dramatically sprang into life.

Extract of the RAF Operations Record Book. Form 540
Held at the Public Record Office, Kew, Surrey.

19.8.42. This was surely the most glorious page to be written in the history of RAF Friston and the events crowded into this one day more than compensated for the many days of comparative inactivity. The majority of personnel on the camp were up and about at 03.00 hours and both squadrons were airborne at 04.50 flying out to sea. It became apparent quite early that the day would see much aerial activity and from this time onwards the sky was never empty. Heavy explosions were heard from across the Channel and both squadrons had returned by 06.00 hours with the exception of F.O Seal of No 223 Squadron who was reported Missing.

The squadrons had been engaged in strafing the beaches at Dieppe to afford cover for waterborne troops who were affecting a landing there at first light in what proved to be the biggest combined operation yet undertaken by the three Services.

At 06.00 hours many aircraft of Fighter and Bomber Commands were passing over the aerodrome on their return to their bases and one Blenheim of No 614 Squadron operating from Thruxton circled several times before making a belly-landing. Unfortunately the load of smoke bombs had not been jettisoned and the aircraft immediately burst into flames. The pilot and navigator were able to get out of the machine, but the rear gunner (who was already dead) was not extricated until after the machine burnt out. It was subsequently learnt that the navigator died in hospital. Within a quarter of an hour a Spitfire of No 71 Squadron from Gravesend appeared over the aerodrome with smoke pouring out from a glycol leak and this aircraft made a successful landing without mishap.

At 07.38 hours No 32 Squadron were airborne again to attack the beaches to the east of Dieppe, all their aircraft returning by 08.45 without loss.The pilots reported heavy fighting

A rare photograph of a Hawker Hurricane IIc (P2865?) with a gathering of Hawker staff. The aircraft bearing the legend The Last of the Many! (Gote House)

on the beaches with the town itself hidden in smoke. At 07.50 a Spitfire of No 332 Squadron (Norwegian) from Manston made a successful landing at Rodmell, near Lewes, after being pursued across the Channel by two FW 190's. The pilot escaped with bullet wounds in the leg and was forced down through lack of petrol when his tank was holed by enemy bullets. The necessary crash party was despatched from this aerodrome.

At 08.00 hours a Hurricane of No 87 Squadron at Charmy Down crashed at East Dean near the aerodrome after the oil tank had been punctured by machine gun fire. This machine was very badly smashed up and the pilot escaped miraculously with nothing worse than a shaking up. The guard for this machine was provided by the RAF Regiment, No 2793 Squadron at Friston.

At 09.23hours a Mustang from No 239 Squadron at Gatwick force-landed at the aerodrome very successfully with smoke pouring from an oil leak caused by enemy action. The airscrew stopped dead over the aerodrome perimeter and the pilot was fortunate to have reached the runway.

The next sortie was made by eight aircraft of No 253 Squadron which took of at 10.00 hours to attack the beaches again, this squadron being unable to raise any more serviceable aircraft. All eight returned one hour later, well pleased with their efforts. At 11.37 hours No 32 Squadron took off again at full strength making a further attack on their original objective, during which two of their aircraft collided in mid-air.One was able to return with one wing tip sheared-off, but the other flown by Flt Lt Conelly crashed into the sea, the pilot being unable to get out in time.

The last sortie of the day from this aerodrome was at 13.05 when No 253 Squadron took off, including four aircraft borrowed from No 32 Squadron. During this trip Flt Lt Ellacombe DFC was attacked by enemy fighters and forced to bale out in the sea near some of the returning barges. He was picked up safely and subsequently landed at Newhaven after being subjected to several dive-bombing attacks and low-level strafing without result.

At 16.10 hours a Spitfire from No 350 Squadron at Redhill force landed on the aerodrome without mishap, after the oil system had been damaged by the explosion of the first cannon shell fired by the pilot.

The last casualty of the day was reported when a Spitfire from No 121 (Eagle) Squadron at Southend crashed near Burwash at 17.50 hours and a crash party was sent out. In this case the engine cut out and the pilot baled out leaving the aircraft to crash on empty field, where it immediately caught fire and was burnt out, the engine being buried eight feet into the ground.

Finally at 18.45 hours, four Hurricanes of No 32 Squadron, were airborne to patrol over the returning barges which were now nearing port, but when they landed at 19.20 hours the weather closed right in and rendered further flying impossible from this aerodrome. This was perhaps fortunate in some respects as it probably prevented bombing attacks on the aerodrome and the neighbouring port of Newhaven where large numbers of the land forces were being disembarked.

By nightfall, eight stray pilots had been fished out of the sea were comfortably installed in the Officer's Mess and sundry others who had force-landed earlier in the day had by then been ferried back to their units. During the days activities 37 visiting aircraft had been refuelled and 4,925 gallons of petrol consumed. The two squadrons based at Friston had between them accounted for 12,858 20.00mm cannon shells and 31,454 rounds of .303 machine gun ammunition.

From dawn until dusk the ground staff had worked with the greatest enthusiasm and efficiency to keep all aircraft possible in the air and Operation *Jubilee* caused great jubilation amongst them. Their keenness to assist in dealing blows attacking the Hun was patently obvious and although feeling tired at the end of the day they unanimously expressed hope that there would be many more such occasions to come.

Top: A Supermarine Spitfire in graceful flight. (Gote House)

Middle: A venerable Avro Anson in its prime. (Gote House)

Lower The second prototype Firebrand TF III taxis during assessment. (Gote House)

Top: A prototype Mitchell II Double Cyclone bomber, seen in October 1942. FL191. (Gote House)

Middle: A Boston Double Cyclone III, seen in September 1942. W8315 of No 88 Squadron survived the war, only to be wrecked 9 October 1945. (Gote House)

Lower: Douglas C54 Skymaster, with Pratt & Whitney engines, poses in August 1944. EW999. (Gote House)

Above: The Douglas C-47 Dakota - the legendary workhorse of the 1940s. Many were ferried to the UK via Montreal and remain in use on civilian routes. (Gote House)

Opposite: An awesome Handley-Page Halifax BII heavy bomber of No 35 Squadron. (Gote House)

Below: The outline of the Liberator bomber became familiar over Europe. (Gote House)

Top: A little known mid-1937 view of Consolidated PBY-2 Catalina 11-P-11. (Gote House)

Middle: RCAF Lancaster 104 of the Maritime Air Command. (Gote House)

Lower: Floatplanes have particular uses in remote Canadian terrain. A 1950s DHC-3 Otter of the RCAF is seen here. (Gote House)

Mainland Exercises

The culmination of a number of exercises encompassing the Canadian Corps began in 1941. Exercise *Waterloo* was staged by HQ South Eastern Command on 14-16 June 1941 and involved about half of the troops in South Eastern Command.

The prime purpose of the exercise was to train Canadian Corps and the 8th Armoured Division in a mobile counter-attack format. The 4th Corps also took part and there was a 'live enemy' for *Waterloo*. The exercise was held in the central coastal region of Sussex and inland around the South Downs which provided excellent training terrain.

The assumption was that the enemy would make glider landings and parachute descents on the northern face of the Downs, to bolster seaborne landings along the Sussex coast. The 'defending' forces developed an attack fending off 'enemy' positions on the Downs. The aim was to drive the invaders back towards the English Channel in retreat and this operation was ultimately deemed as being successful.

Exercise *Bumper*, from 29 September to 3 October 1941, involved a quarter of a million men and was the largest test of training and logistics to date - indeed it was to be largest exercise ever staged in our nation.

The extensive manoeuvres of Exercise *Bumper* were held north and west of London under General McNaughton's Canadian Corps command in an anti-invasion role. Two army HQs, four corps and twelve divisions (including three armoured) were amassed, along with two army tank brigades and vast numbers of ancillary troops.

General Sir Alan Brooke, C-in-C Home Forces, intended to provide Army commanders with battle conditions for large volumes of troops, similar to what might be experienced in Europe eventually. Enemy landings in East Anglia were deemed to have succeeded and South Eastern Command and the GHQ Reserve were deployed to handle the 'enemy' around the Chiltern Hills, north-west from London. Post-exercise analysis examined the lessons learnt in such conditions and battle-drill for Canadians became a routine function by the end of 1941.

Exercise Spartan 1943

The exercise coded *Spartan* assembled from 26 February 1943 and started on 1 March, under the auspices of GHQ Home Forces. However the Canadian 1st Division were excluded from participation due to their combined training roles. Ten divisions took part, compared to a dozen divisions in *Bumper*.

On 15 January 1943 HQ 2nd Canadian Corps had been created and four days later General McNaughton agreed with GHQ Home Forces that the new Corps should participate in *Spartan* with 5th Canadian and Guards Armoured Divisions under his command. It was thought this hasty inclusion might create problems, due to HQs, detachments, vehicles, supplies and signals, not being in place in time. Such trials however may be deemed too realistic to battle conditions and duly added to the offensive circumstances. The logistics of armies on the move were tried to the fullest and the tactics and tensions of war-gaming tried in earnest. Cease-fire was signalled on the morning of 12 March.

In his summary General McNaughton noted that one major outcome of the offensive was the role of aerial support for troops in the field. A mobile composite of 19 RAF and RCAF squadrons had co-operated with McNaughton's planning. This was the first time in the UK that air support, tried out so successfully in North Africa, had been involved.

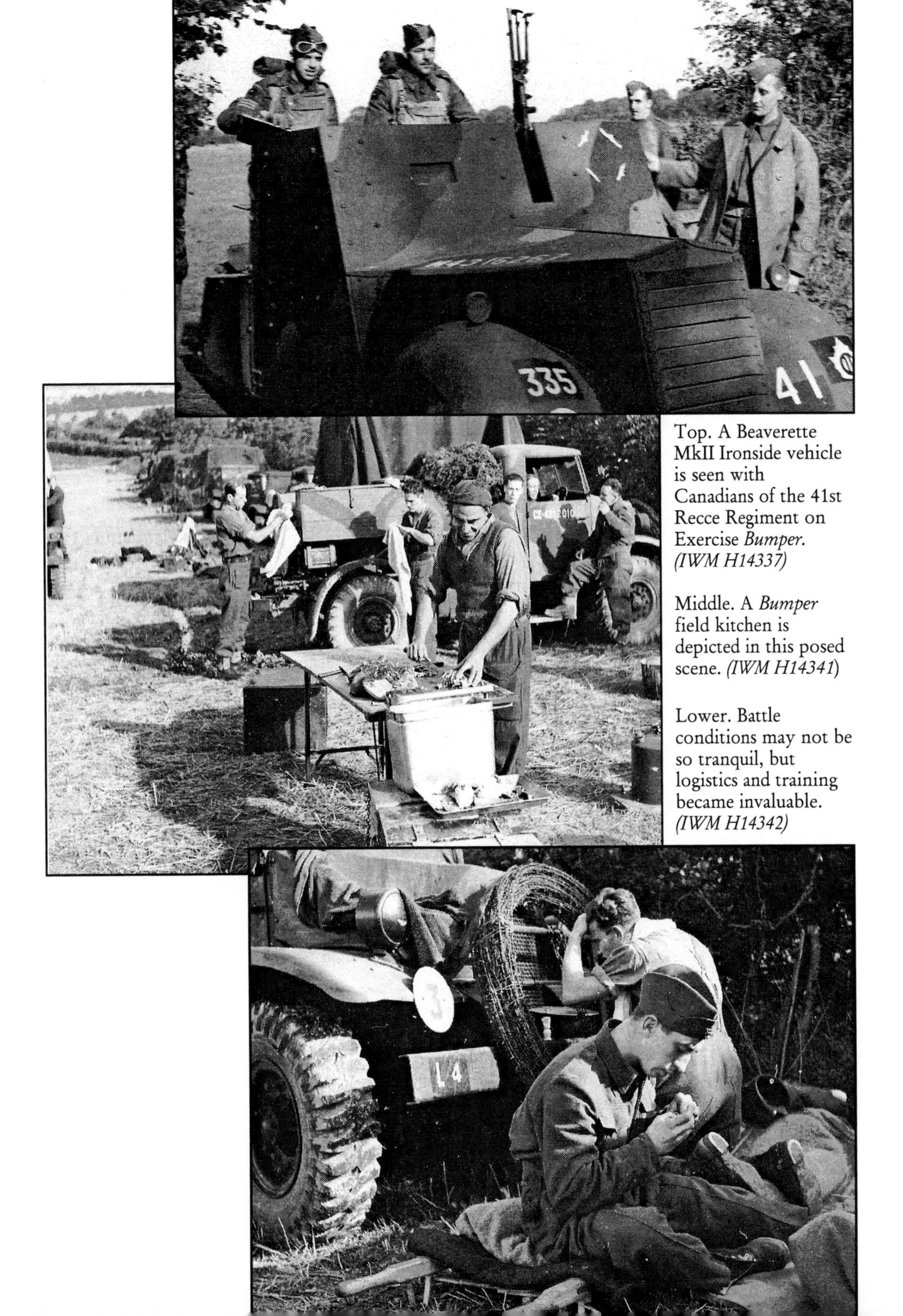

Top. A Beaverette MkII Ironside vehicle is seen with Canadians of the 41st Recce Regiment on Exercise *Bumper*. *(IWM H14337)*

Middle. A *Bumper* field kitchen is depicted in this posed scene. *(IWM H14341)*

Lower. Battle conditions may not be so tranquil, but logistics and training became invaluable. *(IWM H14342)*

Exercise Spartan 1943

Top: Mobile forces were provided with stimulating newspapers during major operations . *(IWM H27825)*

Middle: The censor boobed slightly with this scene relating to an Oxford location. *(IWM H27933)*

Lower: Somebody, somewhere, might be able to trace this location in middle England. *(IWM H27835)*

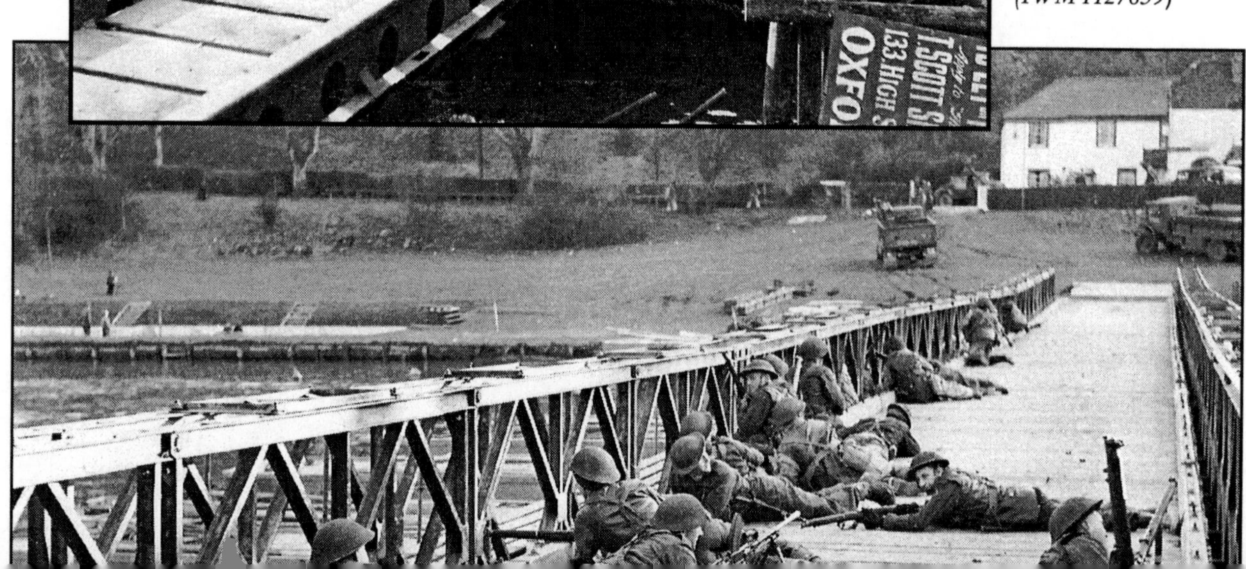

Top: Canadians rarely had problems making friends - as with these youngsters. *(IWM H28023)*

Middle: After frustrating months of inactivity field conditions could be tried. *(IWM H27799)*

Lower: The logistics of an army on the move was one prime factor to test as best as possible. *(IWM H27889)*

Canadian Army badges in World War Two

Military Headquarters, Canadian Forces, UK and Europe.

A golden maple leaf on a black circle, with a gold border.
Set up in 1939 and based in Cockspur Street, near Trafalgar Street, in London. The badge was also worn by UK base units under the command of CHQ.

1st Canadian Army

Formed in England 6 April 1942.
The arm insignia was scarlet horizontal diamond with a broad blue band through the centre.
On vehicles, and directional signs, a yellow maple leaf on a red background with a black strip through the centre.

1st Canadian Corps

A plain horizontal scarlet diamond arm patch was worn.
The 2nd Canadian Division arrived in the UK by December 1940. It was formed to command the 1st and 2nd Canadian Divisions in South Eastern Command in England. They went to Italy in 1943 and fought at Cassino - through to Holland.

2nd Canadian Corps

A dark blue horizontal diamond was worn.
The 2nd Corps was raised in England in 1942. They took part in the Normandy landings, through to the Rhine and onto Holland.

1st Canadian Division

The arm badge was a solid red horizontal patch.
They arrived on the Clyde in Scotland, in December 1939 with a strength of 7,500 officers and men. These men were the first of 335,000 Canadians who came through the UK in the Second World War.

2nd Canadian Division

A Royal blue patch was worn.
This division arrived in the UK in the late summer of 1940 and became based in Surrey and Sussex. They took part in Operation Jubilee. After their Dieppe Raid losses they returned to the UK in 1944 and took part in the Normandy and Falaise actions.

3rd Canadian Division

A grey arm patch was worn.
They came to England, after leaving Canada in July 1941, and took part in the Normandy landings.

4th Canadian Division

A dark green patch was worn.
They arrived in England in the autumn of 1942 and took part in the Normandy landings and then through to Holland.

5th Canadian Armoured Division

A maroon patch was worn.
They left Canada in June 1941 and stayed in the UK until autumn 1943. They then went the Mediterranean. The division landed in Naples in November and finally went through to Holland.

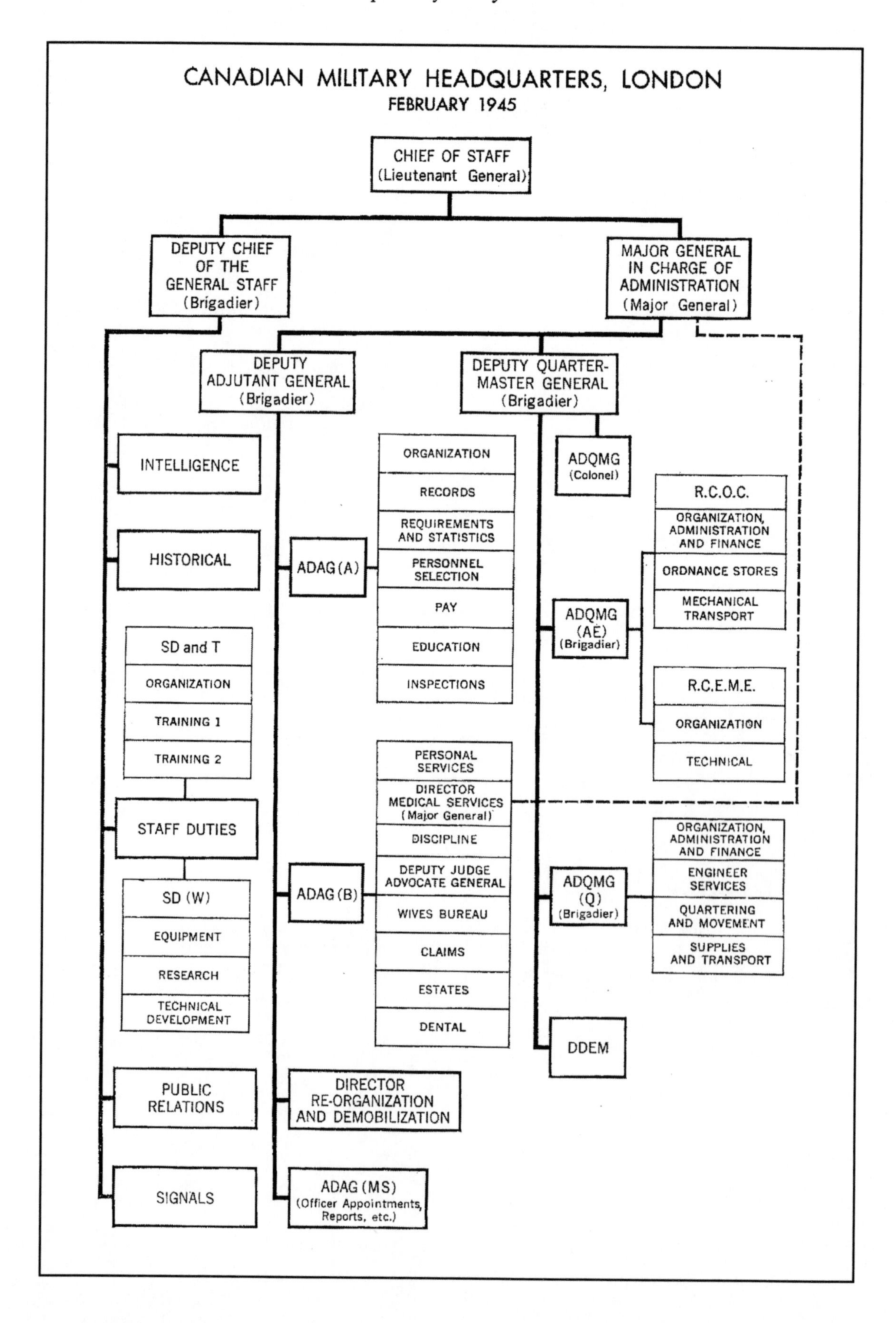
CANADIAN MILITARY HEADQUARTERS, LONDON
FEBRUARY 1945
CHIEF OF STAFF (Lieutenant General)
DEPUTY CHIEF OF THE GENERAL STAFF (Brigadier)
MAJOR GENERAL IN CHARGE OF ADMINISTRATION (Major General)
DEPUTY ADJUTANT GENERAL (Brigadier)
DEPUTY QUARTER-MASTER GENERAL (Brigadier)
INTELLIGENCE
HISTORICAL
SD and T
ORGANIZATION
TRAINING 1
TRAINING 2
STAFF DUTIES
SD (W)
EQUIPMENT
RESEARCH
TECHNICAL DEVELOPMENT
PUBLIC RELATIONS
SIGNALS
ADAG (A)
ORGANIZATION
RECORDS
REQUIREMENTS AND STATISTICS
PERSONNEL SELECTION
PAY
EDUCATION
INSPECTIONS
ADAG (B)
PERSONAL SERVICES
DIRECTOR MEDICAL SERVICES (Major General)
DISCIPLINE
DEPUTY JUDGE ADVOCATE GENERAL
WIVES BUREAU
CLAIMS
ESTATES
DENTAL
DIRECTOR RE-ORGANIZATION AND DEMOBILIZATION
ADAG (MS) (Officer Appointments, Reports, etc.)
ADQMG (Colonel)
ADQMG (AE) (Brigadier)
R.C.O.C.
ORGANIZATION, ADMINISTRATION AND FINANCE
ORDNANCE STORES
MECHANICAL TRANSPORT
R.C.E.M.E.
ORGANIZATION
TECHNICAL
ADQMG (Q) (Brigadier)
ORGANIZATION, ADMINISTRATION AND FINANCE
ENGINEER SERVICES
QUARTERING AND MOVEMENT
SUPPLIES AND TRANSPORT
DDEM

Regimental Insignia

The Corps of
Royal Canadian Engineers

The Royal Canadian
Artillery

The Royal Canadian
Army Service Corps

The Royal Canadian
Corps of Signals

The Royal Canadian
Ordnance Corps

The Royal Canadian
Army Pay Corps

The Royal Canadian
Army Medical Corps

Royal Canadian Electrical
and Mechanical Engineers

The Canadian
Army Dental Corps

The Canadian
Forestry Corps

Royal Canadian
Army Veterinary Corps

Royal Canadian
Mounted Police

The Canadian
Provost Corps

The Canadian Postal Corps

Canadian General Service

Corps of Military Staff Clerks

Veterans Guards of Canada

Royal Military College

Canadian Intelligence Corps

Canadian Armoured Fighting Vehicles Training Centre

Royal Canadian Armoured Corps

Canadian Chaplain Service

Christian

Jewish

Canadian Infantry Corps

The Garrison Battalion (Inf.)

Canadian Parachute Corps

Canadian Technical Training Corps

Lord Strathcona's Horse
(Royal Canadians)

The Royal Canadian
Dragoons

The Governor General's
Horse Guards

First Hussars of Canada

2nd/10th Dragoons

6th Duke of Connaught's
Royal Canadian Hussars

The Prince of Wales's
Rangers (Peterborough Regiment)

4th Princess Louise's
Dragoon Guards

7th/11th Hussars

8th Princess Louise's
New Brunswick Hussars

8th Princess Louise's
Hussars

12th Manitoba Dragoons

15th Canadian Light
Horse

Saskatchewan Horse

17th Duke of York's
Royal Canadian Hussars

The Manitoba Mounted Rifles

19th Alberta Dragoons

14th Canadian Light Horse

8th Reconnaissance Regiment

The British Columbia Dragoons

British Columbia Hussars

The Fort Garry Horse

The Prince Edward Island Light Horse

2nd Armoured Car Regiment

The Essex Regiment (Tank)

1st Canadian Armoured Personnel Carrier Regiment

The New Brunswick Regiment (Tank)

The Governor General's Foot Guards

The Royal Canadian Regiment

Princess Patricia's Canadian Light Infantry

Royal 22nd Regiment

The Canadian Grenadier Guards

The Queen's Own Rifles of Canada

The Victoria Rifles of Canada

The Black Watch of Canada (Royal Highlanders)

The British Columbia Regiment

The Canadian Fusiliers (City of London Regt)

The Royal Rifles of Canada

Les Voitigeurs de Quebec

The Royal Regiment of Canada

The Irish Fusiliers of Canada (The Vancouver Regt)

The Queen's York Rangers (1st American Regt)

The Royal Hamilton Light Infantry (The Wentworth Regt)

Princess of Wales's Own

The Argyll Light Infantry (Tank)

The Hastings & Prince Edward Regiment

Le Régiment de Levis

Le Régiment du Saguenay

The Lincoln and Welland Regiment

The Lorne Scots (Peel, Dufferin and Hamilton Regt)

The Essex Scottish

The Oxford Rifles

The Algonquin Regiment

The Kent Regiment

The Elgin Regiment

The Middlesex and Huron Regiment

The Perth Regiment

The Highland Light Infantry of Canada

The Grey and Simcoe Foresters

The Ontario Regiment

The Dufferin and Haldimand Rifles of Canada

The Midland Regiment (Northumberland and Durham)

The Brockville Rifles

The Lanark and Renfrew Scottish Regiment

The Cameron Highlanders of Ottawa

48th Highlanders of Canada

The Canadian Scottish Regiment

The Sault Ste Marie and Sudbury Regiment

The Prince Albert Volunteers

The Prince Albert and Battleford Volunteers

The Sherbrooke Regiment

The Sherbrooke Regiment

The Sherbrooke Fusilier Regiment C.A.S.F.

The Royal Montreal Regiment

The Stormont, Dundas and Glengarry Highlanders

The Stormont, Dundas and Glengarry Highlanders

The King's Own Rifles of Canada

Le Régiment de Montmagny

The St. John Fusiliers

The Halifax Rifles

Le Régiment de Chateauguay

Les Fusiliers Mont Royal

The Princess Louise Fusiliers

The Carleton and York Regiment

The West Nova Scotia Regiment

Le Régiment de Hull

The Seaforth Highlanders of Canada

The North Shore New Brunswick Regiment

The New Brunswick Rangers

The North Nova Scotia Highlanders

The Pictou Highlanders

The Queen's Own Cameron Highlanders of Canada

The Prince Edward Island Highlanders

Le Régiment de Joliette

Le Régiment de St Hyacinthe

Le Régiment de Maisonneuve

The Three Rivers Regiment

Le Régiment de Quebec

Les Fusiliers du St Laurent

The Royal Winnipeg Rifles

The Argyll & Sutherland Highlanders of Canada (Pr. Louise's)

Le Régiment de la Chaudiere

The Cape Breton Highlanders

The South Saskatchewan Regiment

The Regina Rifles Regiment

The Lake Superior Regiment

MANITOBA VOLUNTEER RESERVE
EDMONTON FUSILIERS
CANADA
EDMONTON REGIMENT
ROCKY MOUNTAIN RANGERS
KLOSHE NANITH
ONWARD
CALGARY REGIMENT
CALGARY HIGHLANDERS
SASKATOON
LIGHT INFANTRY
NORTH WATERLOO
FIOR GO BAS
TORONTO
CARRY ON
1915-1919
SCOTTISH
THE REGT
SOUTH ALBERTA
THE WESTMINSTER REGIMENT
PRINCE RUPERT REGT. N.G.
VIGILANS
The Winnipeg Grenadiers
The Manitoba Volunteer Reserve
The Edmonton Fusiliers
The Edmonton Regiment
The Rocky Mountain Rangers
The Calgary Regiment
The Calgary Highlanders
The Saskatoon Light Infantry
The Winnipeg Light Infantry
The Scots Fusiliers of Canada
The Irish Regiment of Canada
The Toronto Scottish Regiment
The South Alberta Regiment
The Westminster Regiment
The Prince Rupert Regiment
The Pacific Coast Militia Rangers

The Canadian Flag

Although the Canadian nation has a proud and intriguing past it is perhaps surprising that a national flag was not agreed until 1965.

Post-1919 an upsurge of nationalism led King George V to grant the Dominion a coat of arms, with red and white as official colours, in November 1921. Four years later Prime Minister Mackenzie King appointed a committee to investigate potential designs, but they did not report back. Over the next two decades an almost annual House of Commons debate failed to settle the issue - which rested upon whether a Canadian flag should be free of colonial symbolism. In 1946 another committee presented an emblem bearing both the Union flag and a maple leaf, but this also failed to be adopted.

In 1963 Prime Minister Lester Pearson, with heraldic assistant John Matheson, promoted a flag of three maple leaves on a white centre square with blue bars on each side. Formal debate in London, from mid-1964, was prolonged and rancorous. Finally on 15 December 1964 a proposal was carried by 163 votes to 78. On 28 January 1965 Queen Elizabeth proclaimed that Canada's flag would be red with the proportions two by length and one by width, containing in its centre a white square the width of the flag, bearing a single maple leaf. Under average wind conditions the flag should represent the 23-point sugar maple leaf. John Matheson later commented that it was after great political wrangling that the current flag evolved. (See also page 123)

Abridged: *The Canadian Post*, July 2002.

Above: Unruffled by circumstances, like the Canadian people, the national flag flies over a Dieppe Raid memorial in Newhaven. (Gote House)

Above: The welcoming Canadian High Commission building in Grosvenor Square, London. (Gote House)

Lower: The distinctive Canada Gate at Green Park in London, proudly radiates out towards Buckingham Palace.

Memorials & Commemoration

Green Park, London. Close to Canada Gate opposite Buckingham Palace.
On 3 June 1994 Queen Elizabeth unveiled the distinctive flowing water memorial to 110,000 Canadians who gave their lives in two world wars. The ceremony was attended by members of the royal family, with official Canadian and CVAUK representatives.

Shorncliffe Military Cemetery, West Road, Shorncliffe, Kent. Since 1918 and the first Remembrance Day ceremonies children at Shorncliffe, Folkestone, have honoured the 298 Canadian soldiers resting at Shorncliffe Military Cemetery in West Road. The gathering began in 1919 as a flower service - with posies at the graves. Children then stand alongside each headstone for the moving 20-minute memorial service as a bugler sounds the Last Post. Generations of families have perpetuated remembrance of this period - by 1915 40,000 Canadians had passed through the district.

Crowborough Common Golf Course. Pedestrian access off High Broom Road, Crowborough, East Sussex.
One of the county's worst doodlebug accidents occurred at 6.20pm on 5 July 1944, at the height of the V1 attacks across southern England. Canadian troops camped on the sloping Crowborough Common golf-course were lost when a single V1 bomb struck B Company cook-house just after their evening meal.

Crowborough is some 900 feet above sea level. V1's usually fell when their motor cut-out, but on this occasion the missile struck trees and fell. Seven men of the Lincoln and Welland Regiment died at the time, two soldiers died later, and 17 men were seriously injured. If the bomb had descended half an hour earlier, during the meal, then the casualty figure would have been far greater. The men are buried at Brookwood Military cemetery in Surrey.

On 18 July 1948 the distinctive plaque was unveiled by Sir James Grigg, a former Secretary of State for War. The monument is maintained by Crowborough Town Council.

All Saints Church, Orpington, Kent.

Canada Corner, All Saints Church, commemorates 88 Canadians buried there and the WWI Ontario Military Hospital, Orpington, later No 16 Canadian General Hospital.

Seford Cemetary, Alfriston Road, Seaford, East Sussex.

Each September the Royal British Legion honours 191 Canadians at rest in Seaford. They died from the 1918 *Spanish Flu* epidemic whilst waiting repatriation. See page 11.

Canada Green, Church Road, Crowborough.

Pedestrian access off Church Green, close to All Saints Parish Church. The recent planting of ten maple trees with named plaques, leading to a flag-pole focal point, commemorates the victims of the Crowborough Common golf course doodlebug incident on 5 July 1944.

Newhaven Fort. Fort Road, Newhaven East Sussex.

A symbolic plaque facing the parade ground at the Palmerston period fort was dedicated on the 40th anniversary of the *Dieppe Raid* in August 1982 during a memorial ceremony.

South Way/Beach Road, Newhaven. East Sussex.

Royal Canadian Corps of Engineers memorial. On a well-maintained plot of land on the right at Beach Road, just off the main A259 South Way thoroughfare swingbridge. A Royal British Legion parade each August honours *Dieppe Raid* casualties.

Above and opposite: The flowing water and radial memorials in Green Park, London, unveiled by Queen Elizabeth on 3 June 1994 commemorates 110,000 Canadians who gave their lives in two world wars. (Gote House)

Right: On Crowborough golf course a symbolic epitaph was created for the 5 July 1944 doodlebug tragedy.

Lower: At Newhaven Fort a poignant plaque was installed on the 40th anniversary of the Dieppe Raid.

Below: Alongside Beach Road, Newhaven, there is this tribute to 27 Canadians of the Royal Corps of Engineers lost during the fatal 19 August 1942 actions in France. The site is close to an embarkation point for the attack. (Gote House).

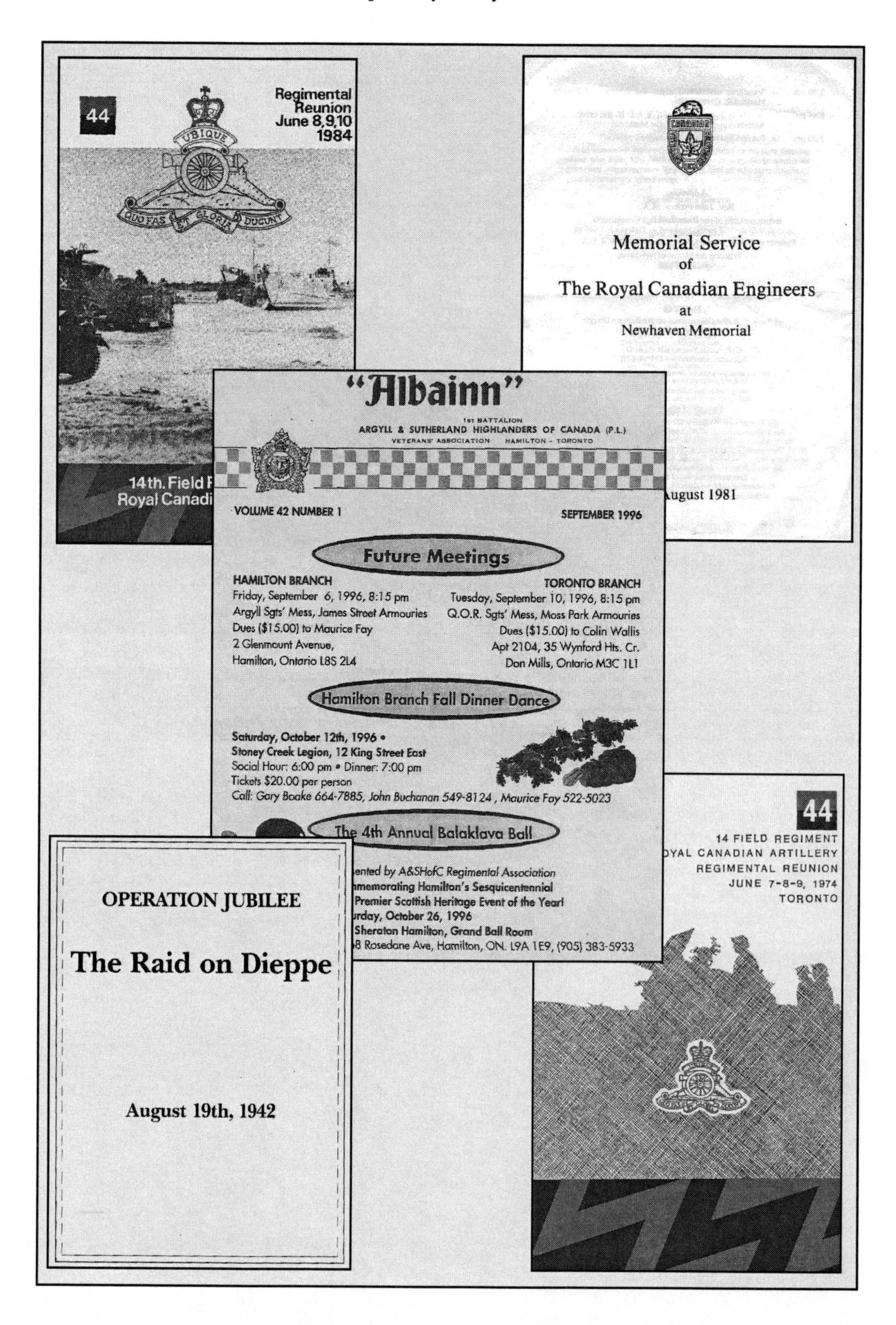
44
Regimental Reunion
June 8,9,10 1984
UBIQUE
QUO FAS ET GLORIA DUCUNT
14th. Field F
Royal Canadi
Memorial Service
of
The Royal Canadian Engineers
at
Newhaven Memorial
ugust 1981
"Albainn"
1st BATTALION
ARGYLL & SUTHERLAND HIGHLANDERS OF CANADA (P.L.)
VETERANS' ASSOCIATION HAMILTON - TORONTO
VOLUME 42 NUMBER 1
SEPTEMBER 1996
Future Meetings
HAMILTON BRANCH
Friday, September 6, 1996, 8:15 pm
Argyll Sgts' Mess, James Street Armouries
Dues ($15.00) to Maurice Fay
2 Glenmount Avenue,
Hamilton, Ontario L8S 2L4
TORONTO BRANCH
Tuesday, September 10, 1996, 8:15 pm
Q.O.R. Sgts' Mess, Moss Park Armouries
Dues ($15.00) to Colin Wallis
Apt 2104, 35 Wynford Hts. Cr.
Don Mills, Ontario M3C 1L1
Hamilton Branch Fall Dinner Dance
Saturday, October 12th, 1996 •
Stoney Creek Legion, 12 King Street East
Social Hour: 6:00 pm • Dinner: 7:00 pm
Tickets $20.00 per person
Call: Gary Boake 664-7885, John Buchanan 549-8124, Maurice Fay 522-5023
The 4th Annual Balaklava Ball
ented by A&SHofC Regimental Association
mmemorating Hamilton's Sesquicentennial
Premier Scottish Heritage Event of the Year!
urday, October 26, 1996
Sheraton Hamilton, Grand Ball Room
8 Rosedane Ave, Hamilton, ON. L9A 1E9, (905) 383-5933
OPERATION JUBILEE
The Raid on Dieppe
August 19th, 1942
44
14 FIELD REGIMENT
OYAL CANADIAN ARTILLERY
REGIMENTAL REUNION
JUNE 7-8-9, 1974
TORONTO

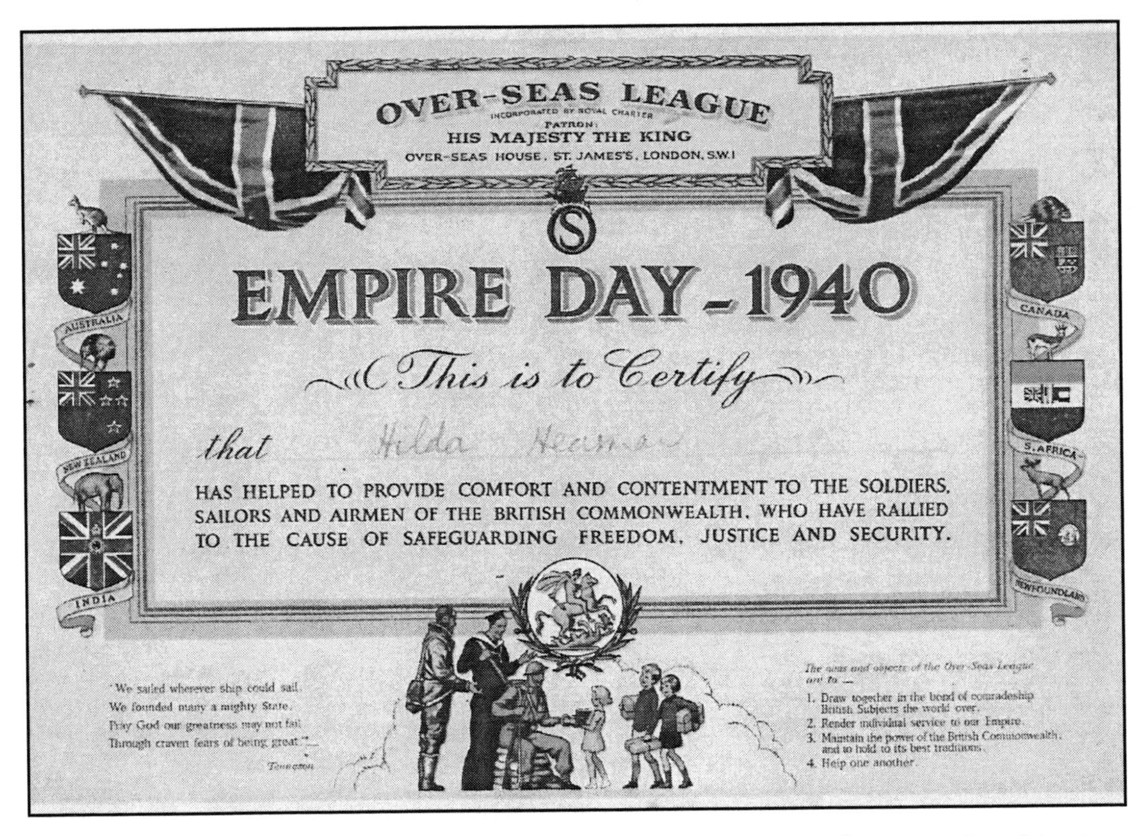

Although the mid-1940s effectively saw the eclipse of the British Empire it was the overseas Armed Services that united to fight alongside Britain - when the aggressor could have all too easily have goose-stepped all over Britain so apocalyptically. (Gote House)

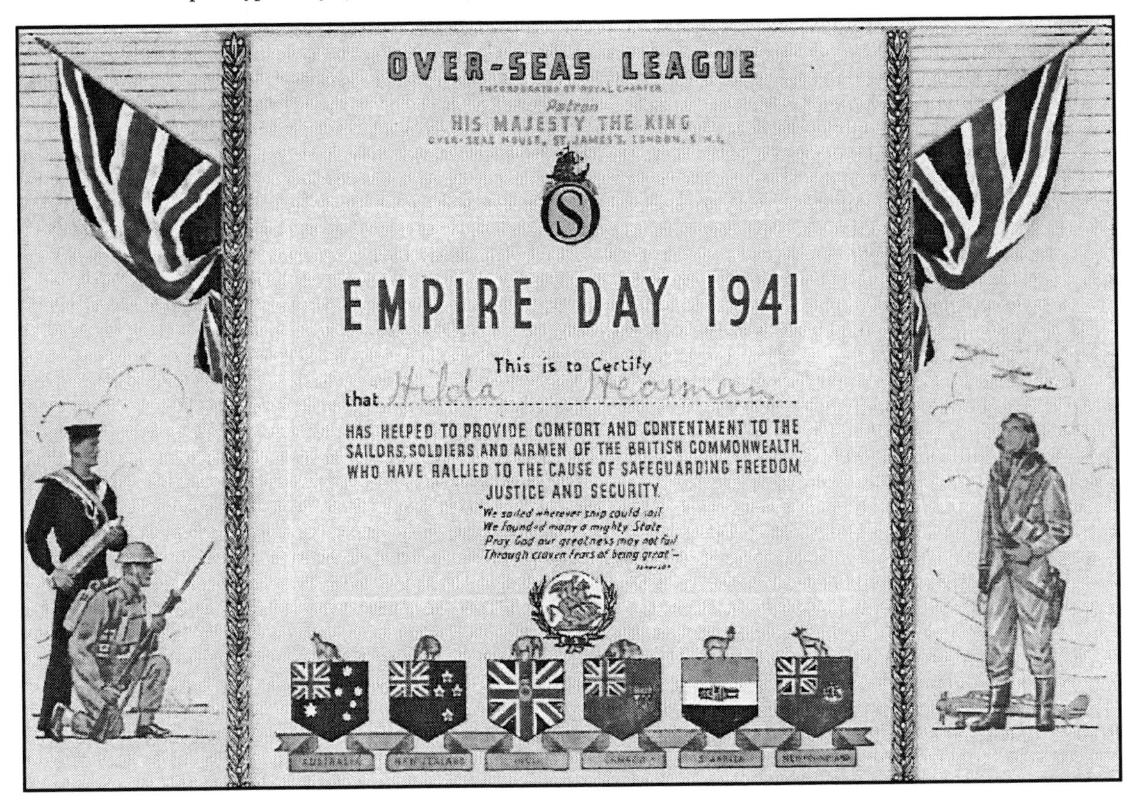

INDEX

Acknowledgments

The authors wish to convey sincere appreciation to the principal contributors, accounts and organisations that have made this archive possible.

Les Edwards, May Jackson, Stanley James, Roger Matthews, Dominic Rumsey and particularly to John Tillstone,

THE CANADIANS IN BRITAIN 1939-1944.
Department of National Defence.
The King's Printers at Ottawa. 1945.

SIX YEARS OF WAR.
Colonel C.P. Stacey. OBE
Queen's Printer and Controller of Stationery,
Ottawa. 1955.

THE HALF MILLION.
C.P. Stacey and Barbara Wilson.
University of Toronto Press, Toronto. 1987.

THE IMPERIAL WAR MUSEUM.
London SE1 6HZ, England.

Back cover montage - clockwise.
'Gunner Kenny' page 40. Phyllis and Harold Grover page 62.
Green Park Canadian memorial page 119. Travers Cosgrove page 14.